Shattered Pieces

BY

Angela Parker

Dedication

To my Oma, who will always have a special place right here in my heart.

Introduction

What you are about to begin reading is not a story of fiction, but rather, a true experience in the life of Angie Parker, myself. What you are about to embark on is a journey into the deepest parts of my soul and innermost thoughts. It is a journey through turmoil and tragedy, in the hopes of giving a better understanding of the slow process of recovering and rebuilding. These are my thoughts and my feelings, put into words and written on paper. Feelings that are very real, raw, and truthful, as well as, powerful and excruciating. In a moment of loss and destruction, this story shows the pain and terror of a traumatic night that would change my life and the lives of many others, forever.

Writing this memory is the only true way that I could help myself to heal the wounds that I suffered, as well as, to give others an understanding as to exactly how it felt and what I saw during the darkest night of my life. I also hope to lend others the strength and courage they need to fight back against this terrible violence that seems to slowly be tearing our world apart.

Before I begin this journey, I feel it is important that I give to you a little background about who I am and how I lived my life. I feel it is only fair, if you are taking this trip with me, that you know something about the person I was before this happened.

I was born October 30, 1975, in Stillwater, Oklahoma. My family moved, in 1983, to a town just outside of Tulsa, called Owasso. My parents separated and divorced when I was seventeen, and I went and lived with my Dad and little sister. April, my twin sister, and truly my best friend who I had never been apart from, moved in with my Mom and we saw one another less and less as that year went on.

In December of 1993, I moved into an apartment in Tulsa and have remained on my own ever since. I worked and finished high school while living in Tulsa too. I moved around a lot during the first couple of years on my own. I was not close with my Dad anymore, after having moved out on my own. He had different ideas for my life, plans I just was not ready for. He never knew exactly where I lived, never even called me to ask or say hello. I never made any effort to tell him either. I did keep in touch with April, Mom and Shauna though, and tried to stay close in the family.

At the time of this incident, that changed so many lives, I was living in a nice, huge apartment in Tulsa, in a "not so great" part of town. I had a roommate, who I had met while working at Waffle House, and I felt like I had a pretty decent life, though not one full of money and expensive dreams. My life was quite simple, and I liked it that way. I was always broke and struggling to make it, but always managed to get by.

My boyfriend, Aaron, who I had been with almost two years, probably was not a good choice for me. We fought almost every day and about senseless things. I loved him though, and at that age, I knew that we would always be together, because I had not lived long enough to really understand. He was all I had wanted in a boyfriend at nineteen, so he was the center of my world.

My life was much like that of any other young, single person. I went out with my friends on the weekends and I stayed out too late sometimes, but I kept away from drugs and alcohol, and I cared a great deal for other people and their feelings.

Preface

I laid on the cold, frozen ground with so much fear in my body that I couldn't even move. I wondered if he was still out there somewhere watching me. I did not feel like moving or breathing, I was so weak and tired from all the blood I had seen and all the fear I had felt.

I laid there and listened so carefully, trying to remain motionless so he would think I was dead. Maybe if he thought I was dead then he would just leave me and run away. Oh, please let him go away and not hurt me anymore.

I heard the car start up and felt the brightness of the taillights through my closed eyes. I lifted my head very slowly, just enough to see if he was going to drive away. The lights of the car were showing he was in reverse. Oh no that meant he was going to run over me. I was going to die after all. Oh, please God let him not do this to me. Then the car went into drive and he was driving away from me. I hoped he would keep going and not stop. I waited, holding my breath, and praying. I saw the car lights going down the dirt road and turn to the left at the end of the street. Soon the car's lights were out of sight and I knew I might be ok.

I put my head back down into the grass and dirt. I felt so numb and stiff and my whole body was aching. I could hardly move as I tried to lift myself up. Having no energy left inside of me, I gave up and laid down again. I wanted to just sleep for a few minutes, so I closed my eyes.

I suddenly realized I had to get up and get somewhere for help. I had no clothes on and I did not know if he would be back for me or not. I was afraid to lay there for too long, so I made myself stand up and walk. My feet were sore and so were my legs. I didn't know where I was because I was so disoriented. It was very dark, no stars or clouds in the sky. I had a pair of socks on my feet and that was all. I didn't take the time to see if my clothes were still there somewhere hidden in the shadows of the trees and tall grass. I did not try to find my glasses either. I just thought about getting help.

I walked down that long deserted road looking for some shred of light to help lead me to a neighborhood. I walked slowly as the rocks and branches along the road were tearing my feet up badly. I made it to the end of the long gravel road and had to decide whether to turn right or to go left. I thought about the direction the man had driven out when he left and began to walk in the same direction. Then I turned back around and went to the right; afraid he might be waiting somewhere in the darkness the other direction.

I began walking down the road. There were some streetlights every so often that helped me to see. I saw a sign that mentioned something about security being in the park at all times, and I thought it was a little funny seeing as how the place looked very deserted. I kept walking.

Suddenly I saw lights, and I tried to figure out what kind of lights they were. Being blind without my glasses especially with it being so late at night, I became afraid that they might be car lights. I jumped into the grass and laid as flat as possible. I felt stickers all over my body, as I realized I must have laid down in a pile of sticker bushes. I laid there for a couple of minutes and realized the lights were not moving. I got back up and tried to get the stickers off of me.

I began walking again, towards the lights that were getting brighter and brighter. When I got closer, I saw that they were streetlights in a neighborhood. I was so happy and so relieved to see them. I looked around trying to decide which side I should go to. I looked for toys or something in the yards, thinking I would be safe with someone who had children.

I began to run, for the first time able to feel my legs. I finally had my first feeling of surviving and I had never been so happy or so relieved to be alive. I ran towards the first house I saw, hoping there was someone home who would help me.

Chapter One

The day was Tuesday, November 28, 1995. I remember it was very chilly that day and the evening was proving to be just as bitter at nineteen degrees. The ground was frozen and covered in a light frost because I remember sliding a bit as I walked. Winter had already made itself at home in Tulsa, Oklahoma. The air was just icy enough to numb your fingers and toes.

I was going to my Mom's house that evening, as I usually did on Tuesday nights. My nine-year-old sister, Shauna, spent every Tuesday evening with Mom, and that was the only chance to see her and to visit with Mom also. Sometimes Shauna would spend a weekend with me though and we would catch up on things.

We had a nice dinner, and afterwards we sat around the table and talked and laughed and just had a great time being with each other. Dad would be picking Shauna up at 9:00pm, so she was running around getting all her things together. Once Dad had come and picked her up, I decided to get ready to go home too. Mom and I had plans to get up early and go Christmas shopping the next morning. I knew I needed to get some sleep before then.

I gave Mom a hug and kissed her goodbye. She offered me a pack of cigarettes, but I said no. She didn't want me stopping off somewhere late at night. She always told me it wasn't safe to be out alone. You know, things a Mom will always say. I told her not to worry, that I could get more in the morning before we went shopping.

I always enjoyed the drives home from Mom's. Mainly because it was quiet, everything would just feel peaceful. I turned the radio to a 70s and 80s station and sang along to most of the songs that came on. I was a bit of a wizard with words and songs. I knew them all. These drives always gave me time to put into perspective all the things that had happened that day. I felt very content and happy that night.

I made it back to my apartment at about 10:00pm to find it dark. Shad, my roommate must have been working the over-night shift at Waffle House. That was okay with me because it meant that I had the place to myself and could clean and pack. I figured I should take advantage of the time I had since he would not be home until seven in the morning. After cleaning the apartment, I went to work packing some of my clothes, dishes, and other belongings, into boxes. I was in the process of moving and up until then I hadn't even begun to get ready for the move. The holiday put me behind some.

I finally wore myself out and went in search of my cigarettes, when I remembered that I didn't have any. I looked up at the clock and it was past midnight. I was exhausted but I just wanted a cigarette, and if you smoke you understand that. I grabbed my keys from the table and did not even bother locking my front door, since the store was so close. I drove down to the convenient store.

I pulled into the parking lot, which was completely empty and deserted at that time. I sat in my car counting out change because I was broke until Friday when I got paid next. Once I had enough change, I went inside. I said hello to the guy work-ing, he was cleaning the hot dog machine towards the back of the store. I could not remember his name, but I recognized him from several other occasions. I asked him for the cheapest pack of cigarettes they had, and he handed me a pack of Austin Lights. I handed him my handful of change to count and then said good-night before heading towards the door.

I saw the clerk go back to cleaning the hot dog machine as I began to leave. I had just gotten to the door when I heard someone yell 'hey' from inside the store near the magazines. Naturally, I turned to see who it was and what he wanted. I turned around and saw a man standing just a few feet inside the front door by the magazine racks. I had seen him standing there earlier when I went into the store but hadn't paid attention to him. Now, the man looked right at me and I began to wonder what he needed. So, I asked him. He asked me if I knew how to get to Broken Arrow. Broken Arrow is a small town just outside of Tulsa. I knew little about Broken Arrow, other than where the Vo Tech was, so I asked him to be more specific and tell me what area. He wanted to know if I knew how to get to 111th and 161st. I knew the approximate location because I was at 41st and 129th now. I began to give him directions on how to get there. He interrupted me saying he did not have a car to get there.

I already knew what he was going to ask me, and I really hoped he wouldn't ask because I just wanted to go home. He asked if I could give him a ride out there, to his sister's apartment. I did not want to drive all the way out there because it was like 10 miles and I wasn't sure of that area. Plus, I was tired, it was freezing outside, and I did not have a lot of gas. I had planned to stop into Waffle House before going home maybe, to say hi to Shad and possibly do some writing. I didn't answer him right away because all those thoughts were going through my head about being tired, wanting to go write and being broke. Then, I looked him over, trying not to be too obvious but I'm sure I was. He seemed to be okay. He was dressed nicely from what I could tell or see under the heavy coat. He was a tall man with a strong build, well-spoken and polite to me, which was rare for a guy in Oklahoma. I made my decision and decided to help him out. After all, I figured I was doing my good deed for the day. And I could always go to Waffle House after I dropped him off at his sister's, if I wasn't too tired.

I told him I would give him a ride and the man thanked me repeatedly for helping him out. I told him it really was not a problem and I was glad to be able to help. He thanked the clerk, who was still cleaning the hot dog machine, and we stepped outside into the freezing night. As we walked to my car, I had a funny feeling inside, but I did not know what it was or why I felt it, so I ignored it. It was bitter outside and I hadn't grabbed a coat when I left the apartment because I didn't know it would be so cold or that I would be out driving around. The wind had picked up though and it was cold, and I hated cold and winter.

I unlocked the doors quickly, and hastily pushed my notebooks and other things out of the passenger seat so he could sit. I apologized for the mess, telling him I was getting ready to move, feeling embarrassed for being so disorganized. I was not big about cleaning my car ever. I hated cleaning and everyone knew that about me. He didn't seem to mind at all though, and he just laughed softly.

He hit his head trying to get in the car and his knees practically touched his chin. It was because the seat was so far forward that his long legs could not fit. I tried so hard not to laugh but I had to turn away and not look at him because it looked hilarious. I pushed the seat back as far as it would go and had him adjust the back. Finally, we were ready to go.

I lit up a cigarette before even thinking to ask him if he minded or if it bothered him. I quickly asked him if it bothered him if I smoked, and he said he didn't mind at all. He said he didn't care about anything right now. I thought it was a strange thing to say so I asked him why nothing mattered, or he didn't care about anything.

I expected him to say something along the lines of it was none of my business, but instead he told me that he had been fighting with his fiancé and she had threatened to call the police if he didn't get out. So, he left before the situation got out of control. He said he was waiting on a cab when I showed up at the convenience store. He told me he had been waiting for over an hour and it never showed up.

I started feeling kind of sorry for him, but also did not really want to get involved in his issues. It did sound like he had been having a rough night. I sympathized with him having to wait on a cab in Tulsa, not only because of this awful cold or the fact that he had been stuck standing in a convenient store, but because cabs were horribly slow in Tulsa and I had been in a similar situation before. I understood the frustration and impatient tone he had in his voice.

I had already begun driving out towards where he said his sister lived. He asked my name and I told him it was Angie. He said his was James. He kept thanking me for the ride and telling me how much he appreciated everything I was doing for him. He said that he had not met very many people who were willing to help other people out. It kind of made me feel good about what I was doing in a weird way, like I was not like every other person he had met. He even offered to give me five dollars for gas, saying it was still cheaper than a cab would have been. I refused to take his money, telling him I understood, even though the money would have really helped me out.

I was very unfamiliar with Broken Arrow other than the Vo Tech that was at 11th and Olive, I think. I had to depend solely on his directions to get to his sister's apartment. I was paying close attention to the streets, names, so that I would be able to find my way back home after dropping him off.

We drove into a nice, little neighborhood called Leisure Park, that reminded me of a place I lived when I was younger. He said we were close because he remembered the elementary school that sat right in the middle of the neighborhood. Still, for knowing where he was, he kept telling me to turn down roads that I could see were dead ends. I saw no apartments anywhere, only houses in this neighborhood. Now he wasn't sure where we should turn next or where we should go. He explained that he had just moved to the area a few months ago, from Michigan.

I suggested that we go and find a pay phone, so he could call his sister and get directions. He agreed, so we began to drive back to an area where I knew there was a Git-N-Go. The radio was playing a Chris LeDoux song and I started to sing along. Music takes me away from frustration, anger, uneasiness, and turmoil. The song playing reminded me of Aaron, who was at home, sick. Aaron loved Chris LeDoux. I loved Aaron so much it felt unreal. I couldn't even make anyone understand my feelings for him.

I started talking about Aaron to this man, and he reached over and turned off my radio. It took me by surprise and made me mad. Considering, it was my car and my radio, and I was being nice, taking him home, I felt like he should have asked before just turning off my radio. I was, to be quite honest, in an unbelievably bad mood and the music was, at the very least, diverting those feelings. The weather was horrible, very cold and driving him around looking for his sister's apartment was not supposed to take so long. I was too tired to even try to bring up how I felt, in that moment. I was just sick of driving and wasting all my gas. I just wanted to go home.

Then, he said he knew where there was a gas station that was closer than the one I was going to. He said it was a Total on 131st. So, instead of going to the place I knew of, I went to the one that he said he knew of, that was closer. As we drove along the dark roads, it seemed like we were getting further and further away from town and civilization. The streetlights were getting farther apart, and roads were darker. It was all just much more secluded then it had been earlier, and it felt scary being out there in this unknown part of town with a guy I did not even know.

After about five or ten minutes, I saw the gas station he had mentioned to me. It sure did not look like much of a gas station from what I could see. There were zero lights on inside the store and it looked pretty run down, like it had not been open in quite some time. I decided it was not in my best interest, or wise, to stop there, and I opted for a place with some sign of life to it.

I was starting to get that uncomfortable feeling in the pit of my stomach. The kind of feeling that you might get when God is supposedly talking to you. I tried to ignore it, bury it, telling myself that I was being silly and way overthinking the whole situation. What could possibly happen? This man seemed to be nice enough and just needing a ride to his sister's.

The guy seemed to be a little uncomfortable himself. I assumed he was probably feeling bad about the situation, too. He started to look around and told me he thought the area looked familiar, so I slowed down a little and started looking for apartments. It was very dark outside, and it made things difficult to see. I was still nervous about driving a stranger around, to spite my efforts to reassure myself. It was obvious, by the way I kept accidentally running right through stop signs. He kept telling me to watch out or I would get pulled over.

He said the road ahead looked familiar, it was Beech Street, which looked like it went into a new, smaller neighborhood that was still under construction. He tried telling me to turn down this street that didn't have a single house or apartment on it. I stopped and looked through the darkness, down the road, for some sign of anything. I saw only a sign that read 'no outlet' but not a building of any kind, so I told him we should go the other direction.

We drove all through that small, new neighborhood and ended up on a main street called Aspen. I was so turned around now, and I had no idea which direction we needed to go. Something inside of me kept telling me to go left, but, of course, the man who knew nothing wanted me to turn right. He had just been wrong so many times, so I decided to go with my own instinct this time, so I went left.

We passed a couple of old, rundown apartment buildings called Indian Springs, which happened to also be the only apartments I had seen since leaving mine, so I asked him if he thought these looked like the apartments his sister lived in. He said no that he had never seen these apartments before, which told me that he had no idea where we were. I drove down Aspen, which was dark and deserted, and showed little sign of life. We reached the corner of Aspen and 131st, where I saw a convenience store and happily pulled in and breathed a sigh of relief.

He got out of the car to make a call to his sister, and I lit up a cigarette, needing it horribly. I watched the store clerk spraying the parking lot down with water, thinking I hoped it would not freeze and cause more problems for the store. There was a young, black man on the other pay phone, but it looked, to me, like he was waiting on a call and not making one. I thought about going inside to use the bathroom, but the area of town scared me and didn't look very safe, so I decided just to wait in my car. I glanced at the clock in the car and it was nearly one o'clock in the morning. I thought about locking my car doors, leaving the guy at the pay phone, and driving myself back to civilization, home, where it was safe and warm. I wanted to forget this night had ever happened. That bad feeling in my stomach had been getting stronger and stronger and I could hardly stand it anymore. Still, I knew this night wasn't over because I had agreed to help this man, and it was terrible of me to keep thinking all these terrible things. So, I waited for him.

He came back to the car and I asked if he had gotten in touch with his sister. I thought, possibly she hadn't answered because he hadn't been at the pay phone for more than a minute or so. He said that he did talk to her and that we were almost there. She told him she only lived about a mile up the road.

I pulled out of the parking lot and up to the stop sign. He said to turn left, which would put us back on the same road we had just come from. I commented that I must have been wrong earlier, when I decided to go left instead of taking a right, like he had wanted to. The road was dark, and trees created shadows where they lined the street. There were not any streetlights and I could barely see the road we were driving on. It did not help that I was night blind, so it took me by surprise when I came upon the dead-end sign.

Chapter Two

I went into a silent panic. It seemed strange to me that he had been quite sure we were on the right road and yet it couldn't possibly be this road. There was not an apartment in sight. In fact, it was completely deserted, and I saw nothing, anywhere. I was suspicious now and my nerves were shot. I knew something was wrong because I could feel it throughout my body. I kept telling myself not to lose it, that everything was going to be okay. I would be fine, all I needed was to get my car turned around and get off this dead-end road. I could just take this man back to the convenience store at the end of the street and leave him there. His sister lived close, he told me himself, so she could just come and pick him up or he could walk the rest of the way. I was done and not taking him anywhere else. I felt like he had taken me on a ride and maybe he had no home, or even a sister. Maybe he just wanted to drive around and get warm. I had no idea; I did not know anything about this guy or what his story was.

I was burning up, even though it was very cold outside, so I turned the heater off. I lit a cigarette and took a deep breath trying to relax. I began turning my car around slowly so as not to end up stuck in the ditch. He leaned forward and told me to be careful not to get stuck. I was barely holding it together; he was not making me feel any happier about trying to do a nice thing. I kept thinking; he must be thinking about me being a woman driver. He was making me more nervous than I already was, and I just wished he would shut up and sit back and let me do this.

I did a couple forwards and reverses to get my car turned back around in the correct direction and get out of this. It took what seemed like an eternity because I was trying to be extra careful. I didn't want him thinking I couldn't drive, and I certainly didn't need any more advice from him. Finally, I put the car into drive and my foot on the gas. My car didn't move, I heard the engine rev but nothing. I had no idea what the problem could be. Why was I having such horrible luck? I checked to be sure I was in gear and saw that I was in neutral. Okay, so maybe it slipped from drive or I accidentally put it in neutral. I put it back into drive again, put my foot on the accelerator, and from the corner of my eye I watched this guy move my gearshift from drive to neutral. I looked over at him with a questioning glance, and he looked back at me with this weird. Unreadable smile. I put my hand on the gearshift to put it back into drive once again, thinking he was playing around for some reason, because he was just that annoying. He reached out and grabbed my wrist.

A sudden feeling of panic shot through my body and I instantly thought 'no, this was not happening'. Maybe he was trying to be funny, but I sure did not see anything funny about it. That thought came and went very quickly and I began to think about how very stupid I was. I knew better than to ever pick up a stranger, even if it was out of kindness. My Mom had drilled that into me since I was little. I knew how dangerous it could be. Did I think I was truly untouchable?

I looked into his face and saw the white of his eyes, shining so clearly, in the darkness, almost glowing. Those eyes were different. They were not gentle, laughing, innocent eyes, of a man that I had seen only moments before. These eyes were on fire, foreboding, confused and estranged. He was smiling and his white teeth showed beautifully in the dark. His smile was far from beautiful though. It wasn't pleasant or comforting, telling me he was joking with me. Instead it was cold, tight, serious, and sly. He made this low, deep, frightening laugh that sounded like it came from some dark place deep inside of him. I felt the evil pour out of him and consume me, sending chills of terror down my spine. Emotions that I had never felt before were raging through my veins.

At first, I could not scream or utter a sound. It was as if, my voice was gone. Whether it was from the fear or the shock, I don't know. I could open my mouth and the words were there, but I had no voice. It was like my worst fear being realized at that moment. I twisted my wrist free of his grip and pushed my hand down, heavily, into the horn. I suddenly found my voice and screamed as loud and hard as my lungs would allow. I screamed so loud and long that I started to choke and had this itchy sensation in my throat. I kept yelling at him, keeping my hand firmly planted in the horn. I tried to fight him off me with my free hand, just trying to keep his fists from hitting me in the face or maybe just to keep them from hitting so hard. "What the hell are you doing?" "What do you want from me?" The horn was echoing endlessly into the emptiness that surrounded us.

I took my hand away from the steering wheel just long enough to open my door and try to make a run for the store that I figured was about a half mile down the street. He quickly grabbed on to my arm and pulled me back inside of the car. I felt his fingers melting into my skin and I just kept on screaming and choking and trying to pull myself out of his grip.

He was saying things; I was hardly hearing him in my agitation. He was yelling and screaming "what are you doing?" and "shut the fuck up, bitch." I never stopped crying out for help. I know I kept getting louder and louder because I just couldn't stop. If I screamed long enough, maybe someone would finally hear me and come to save me. Or maybe if I screamed enough, he would stop. I never screamed so much as I did that night.

He brought his huge, rough hand across my mouth, trying to quiet my screams. I couldn't breathe with his hands covering my mouth and my nose, so I did what I had to do just to catch a breath and a bit his hand. I bit hard, and I did not intend to stop until I tasted the blood in my mouth. He jerked away just long enough for me to take a breath before he was at it again.

He was violent and raging and angry and big. He grabbed me

like a ragdoll, pulling me towards him, but I was still fighting with all I had in me. He started punching me in the face with his fists. They were so hard and strong. They were powerful punches and each blow hit my face like fire, burning. I was not going to let him win, and I was so scared of what would happen if I gave up, that I couldn't even feel the blows to my face anymore.

He kept pulling on me and hitting me, trying to pull me over into the passenger seat so he could take control of the situation. I felt like a punching bag, but every punch I took drew out a little bit more of my soul. I screamed at him "you asshole, let me go!" He just wouldn't hear me; he didn't want to hear me. He just blocked me out, as if I was nothing, and I felt him ripping me apart.

It was all happening at once, so fast and my head was spinning and everything around me was a blur. I couldn't catch my breath and I was trying to keep on fighting. I had to stay conscious, but I felt myself being smoldered by his fists and his large body. In seconds, he had pulled me over across the car and I found myself sideways in the passenger seat with him on top of me. He was climbing all over me, trying to get into the driver's seat, but I was still fighting to keep him from taking me any further than we were.

My left leg was stuck somewhere in the driver's seat, while the rest of me was in the passenger seat. He was almost completely in the driver seat now. I tried to pull at him as hard as I could to keep him from having control of my car. Suddenly, my head was against the back of the passenger seat and he was pushing on me, with the weight of his entire body. He was smothering me beneath his huge frame and tearing the hair from my head at the same time.

At that moment, everything disappeared, and I thought about God. I felt like God was coming for me and it was my time to go, even though I didn't want it to be my time, this was the night I would die. In my mind, I thought, "The Lord is my God" repeatedly. I kept repeating it to myself. I remembered it from the little pieces I had read of the bible in the past. It was only a moment and then I was back inside the car, but it felt like several minutes. I was fighting against the violent nature of this man who had clearly lost his mind. When I came back into reality, though, something had changed in me. I no longer cared what was happening or going to happen in the moments to follow, I just wanted it to be over.

This man was so much stronger than I was. Physically, he was strong enough to break me in two. Eventually, he made his way into the driver's seat, behind the steering wheel. The place I was desperately trying to fight him from getting into. I knew it wasn't good that he had managed to get there. I was in a bad situation that had just gotten worse, and I had little hope left. I felt a sudden sear of sharp pain race through my left leg and realized it was twisted up underneath him, so he was sitting on it, upside down. I turned my body towards the front of the car and unlocked the passenger door, not even caring if he saw me do it or not. I pushed the passenger door as far opened as I could, and he immediately leaned over me and tried to reach for the door and pull it shut. But I had flung my body out into the night so he couldn't close the door without smashing me in it. I tried to pull my left leg out from under him so I could get out of the car while he was driving, but my damned leg wouldn't move. I really didn't care if I had to rip it apart, I was not going to let him drive me another location. I had my entire body hanging out of the car door and my head was inches from the road below. He was swerving all over the road, trying to get me back in the car. If he wanted my car, just let me out and take it. I kept pushing his hands away and was fighting relentlessly, for a while, just to be able to breathe the cold air outside. I knew I wasn't going to be able to get away, but the air felt needed on my face, after being beaten and hot and smothered by him, in the car.

I kept screaming for someone to help me, but no one heard me. I had been very aware of my surroundings and there was nothing out here. I saw no streetlights, no cars, and no people. I screamed until I just didn't have any energy left. I felt lifeless and weak and my throat was hurting. I didn't even have the stamina to try anymore. My screams had become weak and pointless. Eventually, I noticed they had become just small, silent sobs and pleading words, with a man who did not care. I felt there was nothing else I could do to get out of the car or away from this stranger and the danger that I was facing. I was there with no place to run and knew I would be killed … for nothing.

In one final effort to get away, I reached across the car and grabbed the steering wheel, hoping it would cause him to lose control of the car and either slow down or wreck. He hit me and an intense pressure spread through my face. My nose and eyes felt heavy and thick, almost as though they would explode. He continued to hit me again and again, with more and more force. Blood was everywhere I turned, and as I touched my nose, blood ran down my fingers and hand. My head was pounding unbearably, and my nose was throbbing. Everything around me began fading in and out. He continued with the hitting and I feared it would not end until he had killed me. I was in unbelievable pain and confusion and everything seemed to spill together around me. I didn't think I was too far from dying. I couldn't keep up with everything. I did not understand it all.

I just couldn't stop the pain, and I was aware of the tremendous amount of swelling in my face. I kept thinking; this must be how women felt when they were beaten by their husbands. I finally understood how they felt inside and why they felt so empty. All the hurt and not understanding and wondering what they had done to cause this.

My crying was senseless, he wasn't going to stop hitting me, and all my fighting was only making him angrier. I was no match, at all, for this man, not with all his rage and carelessness for my feelings. I saw the blood soaking into the upholstery of the seats. It covered everything around me, and on me, it made me nauseous and weak and tired. I could smell the blood, the sweat, the anger, and emotion in the car. I was terrified, it made me numb and dead inside. I tried telling myself that all of this, that was happening, was a dream. It wasn't real and I would wake up from this nightmare soon. I was just so confused by it all. Deep inside I knew it wasn't a dream. I knew it was real and I was dying.

His fists hit me like fiery explosions on my skin. I felt it breaking my skin and leaving deep cuts in my face. The warmth of my own blood ran down my face and into my mouth. The pain pulsated like it had its own heartbeat. I felt the heat, the burning, and the tightness all over. My tears burned as they soaked into my open wounds. There was no way I could get away from this man and I felt myself giving up and giving in.

I began to think about how I had gotten into this situation in the first place and thought about how stupid I was to believe this man needed help and I could help him. No one would ever believe me if I lived to tell this story to them. Not many people help someone just to help them. Then I started thinking that I might not live to see my family anymore.

I couldn't breathe and I knew I was hyperventilating. I tried to concentrate because I needed to do something to calm myself down or I was going to pass out, and if that happened, there would never be a chance of getting through this. I couldn't calm down though knowing he was going to kill me.

I had to be rational now. I had to start thinking clearly and remember what was taking place. I knew that, in order to remember, I had to calm down. That would be my only chance of survival. It would also give me something to focus on instead of how he was going to kill me. I needed to remember to be strong and remember everything that was happening.

I started taking very deep breaths and I tried to sit up. I had been laying low in the seat and curled up into myself, just to be small and protect myself from his punches. I knew I had to sit up, take deep breaths and get myself together. I had stopped fighting, but I was still crying. I had moved myself as far away from him and as close to my door, as possible.

He was still making threats to me, but I ignored what he said, just as he was ignoring my cries and my pleading. His voice was thick with anger and hate. It made me shiver inside, why was he such an angry person? I heard only one thing he said, and strangely enough, it gave me a miniscule amount of hope that I might not be killed. He said if I did not shut up, I would wish I was dead.

Everything that was happening seemed to vanish into some remote place in my mind. It just faded into the background. I was no longer trapped in my car, or in pain, or afraid. All the feelings of being terrified and of dying, just disappeared. I still saw this bloody girl, beaten almost lifeless in the car. Maybe she was part of me, who had ceased feeling or having any emotion or fear at all. She was a part of me who seemed to have no realization of what was happening, and about to happen, to her. Maybe she had simply given up, accepted what was going to happen and was ready for it to end.

I had begun to pray, unable to deal with all the horror. I was unable to take any more violence from this person, so I put it in the hands of God. I was experiencing something I had never experienced before. I had a fear of the worst kind. A fear that I had never felt before, ever hoped to feel, or even knew existed. A fear so direct and real and terrifying that I could not look it in the face. It was the fear of dying. Not just thinking that I might die, but knowing that death was coming, it was inevitable and would happen this night.

I needed strength and courage to face it. I had to accept it because I knew that I could not change it. I felt God surround my body, or what I called God. It was almost as if a wall was being built around me, to keep this man out. It felt like a blanket of protection, of peace. Not like the peace I felt when I was content, happy, but something stronger. It felt like complete inner peace.

The stranger, whose hatred permeated throughout the car, brought me swiftly back to what was happening. I didn't really fear him anymore. It was like I still had some control and understanding inside of me. I knew he held my life in his hands. He reached over and touched me in my private area. I cried and quietly said 'no, no, no' and inched even closer to my door. I tried not to think about what I knew he was going to do to me. I kept telling myself that it wouldn't happen, and he would just kill me without taking anything else from me. I just couldn't accept that he was going to rape me. For some reason, the thought of him forcing himself inside of me, taking the small piece of self that I still had, was just way too much. I kept thinking of all the ways he might take my life from me. Would he just be quick, or would he torture me first?

I pleaded and begged him, offering him anything he wanted if he would let me go. He could have my car, my money, anything he wanted, I just didn't want to die. I remembered hearing somewhere, that if you can make your attacker see you as a person, rather than this inanimate thing that can just be torn to pieces and thrown away, then the attacker might become less violent. I went so far as to tell him I was pregnant, and I was a diabetic, and that I was afraid of passing out or going into convulsions. I tried being practical, telling him I would not tell anyone if he would let me go. I talked to him about God, which I am not very versed on, saying if people were good to one another then God would be good to us and forgive us for our mistakes.

Nothing was reaching this man and, believe me, I was frantically trying things that make no sense. He just drove on, as though he couldn't even hear me. I looked out the window to see where he was driving. I did not recognize anything, but it was a very dark and deserted gravel road, something like a service road, maybe. There was a fence running along the right, passenger side of the road, and trees and bushes along the other side. It seemed to be a straight road, but I couldn't see more than a few feet in front of me. He suddenly came to an abrupt stop, jerking me back into reality. I looked around me, to see what had made him stop so fast. I saw the road just seemed to disappear into nothing. It was almost as though it would fall off the end of the earth. Looking closer, I realized that it disappeared into a body of water.

He quickly put the car in reverse and backed up into a small opening, just before the road meets the water. Beyond the opening, was an area of thick, tall grass and lots of trees. He had to have known how to find this place because it was far too hidden and dark for anyone to just find it driving by. It made me wonder if he had planned this. He shut off the car and turned off the lights. I took a deep breath and knew that my time was extremely near. I had only a few minutes left to live.

He yelled at me to open the door. I didn't move, although I knew I should do what he said, something just wouldn't let me move. Maybe it was shock or fear of losing my life, knowing if I took that next step everything would be over. I was not ready to die. He didn't wait, without hesitation, the stranger climbed over me, opened my door, and jumped out of the car. He then pulled me out of the car by my arm. He then dragged me by my hair until I found myself thrown on the ground.

He started to unbutton his pants, while at the same time, telling me to take off my shirt. I cried out 'no', and he turned to me and with no effort or thought, he grabbed my shirt and pulled, ripping my shirt and my bra completely off. I was shaking, not from the cold, but because I wanted to somehow stop time. I could not bring myself to accept what was happening to me. I hadn't wanted to believe this was really going to happen.

I was never that girl that would expose myself to a stranger the way he was forcing me to. I felt sick, humiliated and, most of all, scared. He yelled at me to take off my jeans, and instead of arguing with him, I slowly started unlacing my shoes. I was doing it so slow, wasting time, trying to put off what was going to happen. I needed to understand, or at least have an excuse, for why this person was doing this to me. I didn't want to die like this, with no respect and no dignity. I needed my dignity, at the very least. I wanted the chance to say goodbye to my family. I didn't want to be found bloody and naked, by some stranger.

He grew impatient with my stalling and he grabbed my foot and yanked my boots off. He kept pulling so hard, my jeans and panties both came off together. He threw them into the tall grass that surrounded us. I had begun to cry and talk hysterically. I was lying there on the cold ground completely naked, except for a pair of purple socks that were still on my feet somehow. I felt sick, embarrassed, alone, and vulnerable. I was this stranger's cheap whore. I kept asking if he was going to kill me and telling him I would do anything if he would just please not kill me.

He pulled my legs, scraping my lower back on the hard ground. He held them on top of his shoulders. I felt so weak and tired, I couldn't keep my legs from falling off, so he deliberately held them there. He was becoming angry. He pushed my legs apart with his arm and then forced his fingers inside of me. I felt it burn as he kept on and on and then I felt pain and my body trembled, as he forced his hand inside of me. I felt him tearing me and I tried so hard not to cry. I didn't want to cry because I didn't want him to know he was hurting me.

The man pulled his hand out and tried to put his penis inside of me, but he couldn't get it in. He backed away and said I was too dry. He was telling me to get wet. Obviously, I couldn't do that, so he began spitting on me and rubbing his hands in it until he felt it was good enough for him. He penetrated me and pushed himself inside me several times, harder and harder each time. I felt the rocks and sticks, as they dug deep, scraping my back. I wanted to be dead. Every single time he thrust harder inside of me, I felt him stripping away a little more of my soul. It was as if he was killing me very slowly and methodically. I did not know how to make it stop. Should I pretend to like this? Should I cry out? I so desperately wanted to. I just wanted this to end.

I felt myself being ripped apart. Everything inside of me was dying. My identity, my self-respect, my soul, even my life seemed to be turning sour and becoming infected with his evil. Everything was being taken from me, in the night. All the hopes and dreams of a good life shattered under the breath of this angry man. All I could do now was lay there and cry silently. I was completely helpless and all that I loved about me and that was mine, had been stolen away. I was invaded, in a way that I could never explain to anyone, and I felt murdered.

He had not stopped raping me, but I had stopped thinking about what he was doing. My mind wandered to better places and I thought about all those moments of my life that brought me feelings of peace. I ached inside, at the thought of never seeing my family again. I would never get to see Shauna grow up or tell my Dad that I love him, and I was sorry for anything I did that hurt him. I would never see Mom or April or tell them that they made a huge difference in my life. I was angry at myself for never telling them how I felt about them. I always thought I would have forever with them, and I would have plenty of time to tell them. But , in just a moment, I realized I had lost all my chances of ever saying anything to them.

The stranger got up suddenly and startled me back into the moment. He had done everything he could possibly do to me, other than killing me, and I didn't feel like the same person I was just hours earlier. I felt like he had taken every piece of me and stained it or tainted it with his evil. He pulled his pants back on and turned to me. I was trying to sit up but was in so much pain that I was struggling. He yelled for me to lay on my back and close my eyes and not open them. I did. I heard him going through pockets and clothes searching for something, but I had no idea what. He had murdered the girl I used to be, and I was weak, tired, and feeling sick. I was ready to die. I just wanted this to be over. I knew I couldn't go through this any longer.

I laid there, on this frozen ground, and prepared myself for what would be my last moment alive. I accepted that, at twenty years old, my life was ending. I tried only to think of the good things through my life and I realized just how I took so many little things for granted. More than anything else in my life, I wanted to live for Shauna, my little sister. I pictured her sweet face, her innocent and happy smile, and the love that surrounded and seemed to flow through her. I thought of her small, little voice and I cried for her. I prayed that God would look over her and let her always remember how much I loved her.

It was with her in my heart and the warmth of her spirit in my soul, that I accepted death. I felt ready now. I was no longer afraid. Because I was going to be brave and strong in my final moments, for my little sister. I would shine because I felt calm and a peaceful feeling inside.

Then, I remember quite well, feeling this presence close beside me, like a warm blanket covering my naked body. My hand was laid out on the ground and I opened my hand and felt this touch of warmth. Maybe it was because of what was going to happen, but I felt like Jesus was lying beside me, holding my hand, and waiting for me. He had taken the pain and the fear from within my body. I felt tranquil and safe, and I knew everything was going to be alright. Jesus was waiting to take me from this place.

The man began kicking me in the head repeatedly. I felt the hard blows, but they didn't hurt me. I felt the pressure and force of his foot kicking my face and head. I knew my face was bleeding profusely but I didn't really have a care in the world anymore. I felt the blood flow from my nose again, and the pressure of the blood rushing into my head. Then my body completely relaxed, and my breathing got incredibly quiet and slow, as though I was whispering where only God could hear. It felt as if I was in some sort of trance.

I wasn't in my body anymore. I was far out beyond it. I saw it laying there on the ground, looking broken and lifeless, but I knew I was not there, and I was, somehow safe. I still felt the stranger, as he picked me up and threw my body over his shoulder. My body felt light and limp and I saw myself slipping further down towards his feet. I didn't care; I only wanted to die now. I had given up long ago and I knew I was taken care of now, and I was ready.

The man was carrying me toward the bank of the river, and I thought he was going to drop me over the edge into the water. I wondered how long it would take in below freezing weather, to die. Then, I felt my body hit the ground hard. Not knowing if I was close to falling into the water, I held tight to the grass underneath me. I clung to those straw-like blades of frozen grass that stung my face and body, using them for their warmth. I laid there, unmoving, wondering how long he would continue to torture me.

I didn't dare breathe, for fear he would see me move. I knew he thought I was dead, but as though to make certain or assure himself, he started kicking me again, over, and over, harder each time, in my head. I never made a sound, never flinched, never cried, or moaned or anything. I couldn't feel anything, anyway. I just let go of my body.

I kept my eyes closed and listened. I could hear him as he walked away, through the crisp grass and crunchy leaves. He was somewhere near the car, picking up clothes from the ground and throwing, what sounded like jeans, into the thicker part of the grass. I assumed he was getting rid of any traces of me. He was wiping clean anything that would say he had been in that field this night, with me. He was trying to cover up the violent acts he had committed here.

I heard his footsteps again, as they drew closer and closer to me. Would this ever be over? Then he stopped. I heard nothing for what felt like minutes, but I could feel the stranger close to me. Was he waiting and watching to see if I moved? He started walking again, but I couldn't tell if he was coming closer or if he was walking away from me, at first.

Then, I realized he was walking away from me, up towards the car. I heard the car door open and the car was dinging. He had left the keys in the ignition the whole time. He started the car, and without moving my head, I opened my eyes barely enough to see if he was really leaving. I saw the car lights go into reverse and immediately thought he was going to run me over. Then he turned on the headlights and started to pull forward, out of the hidden path that he had driven into earlier. I watched as he drove my car down that long, deserted, gravel road. When the lights from my car had disappeared, I put my head down into the grass and I took a deep breath, knowing I would live.

Chapter Three

For a few moments I continued to lie there. I thought about just closing my eyes and sleeping for a little while. I felt so exhausted and weak and sore. I had no energy, not even enough to pull myself up from the ground and find someplace safe to rest. Slowly, I lifted my bloody, beaten, aching body from the ground. I had to get up in case he should come back for me. Grass was stuck in the blood that had dried on my hands, face, and body. I hurt in my private area and my legs, and my face was severely swollen.

I didn't try to find my clothes. I didn't even think to look for them. I could barely see without my glasses, which I had not realized were gone. I simply stood and began walking very slowly. I walked, and I thought, and I cried. I staggered along the gravel road, slowly and painfully. I cried deep and hard, but I cried freely, where that stranger could not see my pain. My legs were weak, and I was in distress. I wanted to sit down or lay down and just cry and close my eyes forever and sleep, to wake and find it all to be a dream. I felt the rocks beneath my feet, and I knew I would have bruises the next day.

I walked so long it felt like eternity. I finally saw lights in front of me, but without my glasses, I could not tell what the lights were coming from. I thought it was a car and I feared it was the man coming back to find me. I ran as fast as I could to the side of the road and lay in the grass hoping I would not be seen. I cried when I realized I had laid down in a sticker patch and had stickers all over me. I looked up after a couple of minutes of not seeing a car drive past and realized the lights were not moving. I got up on my feet and squinted to see what they were from. I cried as I got close enough to see that they were the streetlights from a neighborhood.

I had only a pair of socks on my feet, but I didn't even care. In fact, I had not even really thought about the fact that I was walking completely nude for everyone to see. I feared the stranger would come back at any time, so I ran. I hoped that someone would open their door to me. What if I scared them? I surely could not scare anyone, could I? I was so small, at five-foot-one, to harm anyone.

I ran to the first house that I came upon and I rang the doorbell. I hoped someone would answer the door, knowing it was around one thirty in the morning. I saw people moving inside the house, but no one ever came to the door to help me. A new fear began to arise inside of me. I wondered if no one would open their door to me and the stranger would drive past and see me and drag me back into the car.

I quickly ran to the next house, scared for my life again. I rang the doorbell repeatedly. I was crying and yelling 'please help me!' I saw my reflection for the first time, through their window, and I cried harder. I did not recognize the person who was staring back at me. I was afraid of her. Suddenly, there was a man looking at me through the door and it startled me. I cried for him to please let me in, and he quickly opened the door. His wife was standing behind him, and they pulled me inside.

I had made my way to the home of Lisa and James Frederick. I had walked to safety and they had saved me. Maybe they did not even realize all they had saved me from. They had saved me from my fear, from the stranger, and from the coldest night I had ever known in my entire life.

It was not until Lisa and James opened their door to me that I finally felt a sense of safety. James immediately put his robe around my frail body and then went to the phone to call the ambulance and the police. I was trying to explain to Lisa what had happened to me and that I wanted to call my mom.

She gave me some Kleenex to stop some of the blood that was still coming from my mouth and my nose. She also brought me a container so that I could use the restroom. She said that

I should save the urine for evidence purposes. She told me not to take a shower or wash off because I could wash away fingerprints and other forms of evidence that might be vital.

I went into the restroom and glanced in the mirror. I looked again at the person who stood in front of me. The face looking back at me was one that I had never seen before. This face was swollen and had deep, dark circles under the eyes. I turned away, unable to look any longer at what had been done to me. I felt sick inside. I used the restroom and took the container back into the living room.

I sat on the sofa feeling embarrassed of what had happened. I felt like closing my eyes and letting it all slip away. I knew I would not be able to rest though. I began to tell Lisa what I had been through. I had started shaking because my body was coming out of the shock, and I was feeling just how severe the pain really was.

I wanted my mom to be there so bad. I just wanted to hug her and tell her how much I loved her. I fought back tears as I thought about her. I had called her and told her that someone had beaten me and stole my purse. For some reason I was having a hard time saying the word rape to her. It just hurt too much to say it. Finally, I told her that I had been raped and was beat up really bad and was going to the hospital. I heard a thud and then the phone was silent for a minute or so. Howard came to the phone then and said she was crying and trying to put her makeup on. He said he would help her get to the hospital and I said ok and hung up.

Lisa sat with me until the police got there, which only took a few minutes. The house became very noisy and policemen were running around everywhere. They made sure I was ok and then began their work. They asked me questions about the stranger's appearance and clothing. I gave them as much detail as I could, and they put out an immediate APB (All Police Bulletin) on him. I was asked to tell them everything that had happened as best as I could remember it. I told them everything and Officer Stalling wrote it down as I said it. It seemed to take forever for me to tell the whole story and I later realized it always was hard on me to tell the story in such detail. I was extremely exhausted and drained of all energy, and all I wanted was to see my mom.

All of the police and the detectives were genuinely nice to me and did not rush me or push me, in any way, as I explained what happened. They were patient and let me tell them just as I remembered.

The ambulance came just as the police had finished taking their reports from me. There were so many people everywhere, that I could not figure out what was going on or who was doing what. The paramedics put me on the stretcher and wheeled me out to the ambulance. It felt so good to lay down. Everything was happening so fast that my mind was hazy. I saw people standing all over the front yard but couldn't be sure who they were or why they were there. I looked; thinking maybe my mom was somewhere in the crowd. I never saw anyone who looked like Mom.

I was rushed to Broken Arrow Medical Center, where I was going to have to go through a rape exam. I asked the paramedic if he could help me to wipe some of the blood off of my face before my mom saw me. I did not want to look bad when she saw me, because I did not want her to cry. The blood made it look worse than it was. I knew she would be upset, as it was, I did not want to make it any harder on her.

When the ambulance arrived at the hospital, I was taken into a private waiting area, where a Call Rape advocate, Linda Gaddy, talked with me and helped me to relax before the exam. She explained to me, what a rape exam was used for and about the procedures they would be doing. She also told me about the many services that were available to me through Call Rape.

Mom had not made it to the hospital yet, because when I had called her on the phone, I told her I would be going to a hospital in Tulsa. I was actually taken to a hospital in Broken Arrow because the Tulsa hospital was further away and also didn't do rape exams. The doctor was ready to see me, so I was taken by wheelchair into the X-ray room.

The doctor took x-rays of my face from every angle imaginable and a couple x-rays of the rest of me to see if anything was broken or fractured. Once the x-rays were finished, I was wheeled into the exam room. Linda and a nurse were there, and they talked to me a little bit and tried to explain to me what they were going to do. There were about twenty, small paper bags laid out with labels on them. I would be giving them samples of my hair, skin, blood, spit, and dirt from under my fingernails, as well as doing a full pelvic exam. They would collect these samples for evidence.

I was uncomfortable about having a pelvic exam after what I had just gone through. I didn't really have a choice though. If I wanted to put that man away, I needed the evidence that this would give me. The exam was not so bad though; the only pain I felt was from the pelvic because I was still so sore. The rest of the exam really did not hurt at all. It was a little embarrassing to know that a man had to come in and take photographs of the parts of my body that had been cut, bruised, or showed any type of finger marks. He took pictures of my face, back, private areas, legs, arms, and any other places that they saw marks. Then the nurse gave me medications for preventing diseases and pregnancy. She also wrote about six prescriptions for medications that I would need to begin taking later in the day.

Once the exam was finished, I was wheeled out to the small waiting area where my mom was waiting. She had arrived while I was in with the nurse. When they wheeled me in and I saw her, I could no longer hold back the tears that I had longed to cry. I cried, realizing for the first time, that I had almost died, and how much I loved my family. I saw all that I had taken for granted and never wanted to lose again.

April, my twin sister, was there and so was Aaron. I felt incredibly lucky to have them with me because I didn't feel alone anymore. Mom came over and hugged me and it felt good to me. She told me that it looked like my nose was broken and I told her that no one had told me if anything was broken yet.

I could see the tears in her eyes, and I could not begin to describe the hurt that I felt in the pit of my stomach. I had never felt such a deep, undying, all-consuming love for anyone, as I felt for my mom at that moment. The realization that I had almost lost her forever, and I might never have seen her or April again, hit hard in my heart.

The nurse came back and said the doctor was almost ready to see me, and wheeled me into another room and Mom, April and Aaron followed. The doctor would be in, in a few minutes. Officer Stalling came in and asked if I could start writing my report for him. He gave me the paper and the clipboard, and I wrote a little, while I was waiting for the doctor to come in. I had barely started when Aaron said he was going to be sick again. I told him he didn't have to stay, that I would be fine now. He gave me a hug and said he would call me later, and then he left.

The doctor came in and the first words out of his mouth were that my nose was broken, and I had multiple contusions to my head. He wrote out a couple more prescriptions for pain medications and told me I would feel much worse for the next couple of weeks. He asked if anyone had any questions before saying that I was free to go home.

After the doctor left, Detective Shea came in and told me that they already found my clothes, and he also had a fairly good idea of who had done this to me. He said that he wanted me to come and see him in a few days, to look at some pictures and drive out to the crime scene. I told him that would be fine, and he left.

I finished writing my report and making sure that I had all the information and phone numbers the hospital had given me, before I left. By the time I finished doing all that I had to do, it was almost seven o'clock in the morning. I was lifeless and I figured Mom was too. My whole body had begun to throb, and my face felt very heavy. My lip had been broken open severely and my teeth all along the right side of my mouth had been chipped. I was ready to go home and rest.

Mom took me home with her and I made her walk right next to me out to the parking lot. I locked our doors once we were in the car because I was sure the man was still following me.

I talked to Mom on the drive home and we both cried. Mom didn't pry and she did not think I was crazy for feeling so scared.

When we got home, Mom helped me to lay down on the couch and put ice on my nose. Then she called work to let Howard, her boyfriend, know that we had made it home. She called Grandma and explained what had happened and my grandma said she would drive down. Mom asked if I was hungry and I told her I wasn't sure. She made us lunch and we stood at the counter and laughed because we were eating lunch at eight o'clock in the morning. Time was all messed up for both of us. Neither one of us was really tired anymore.

My grandma drove from Bartlesville, which was about a forty-minute drive, but she seemed to get to our house in just minutes. She and Mom made sure I was okay to stay alone for a few minutes, while they went to the store to get my prescriptions filled. I really did not think anything would happen while they were gone, so I said that was fine. I needed the medications anyway. I was supposed to start taking them immediately and I didn't want to take the chance of getting some sort of infection or disease.

While Mom and Grandma were out, I called my dad. He asked how I was feeling, and I told him that I was hurting pretty badly. He said he tried to see me in the hospital, but the nurse told him I had just left. I told him that I loved him, and he said he loved me too. I let him go because I was tired, and I didn't think I could deal with any more emotional swings. I had an ache inside and was fighting back the tears from hearing him say I love you.

I was exhausted and I laid down on the sofa to rest, but I could not sleep. Each time I closed my eyes I would see that man's face. I was afraid to be by myself and being alone made the house seem to make strange sounds that put me on edge. I could lay my head down, but I would be so tense, and I would not move because I had to listen for sounds of someone being outside.

Mom spent most of the morning calling family and telling them of the horrible tragedy I had just been through. I was glad to let her tell them because I didn't feel like seeing anyone. She would try and explain to them how awful I looked. She and Grandma helped me to get around the house and they brought me pills when it was time for them. I took a shower and I washed myself until I was sore. I was dizzy under the steaming water, but I had to get that stranger's smell and feel off of me. It wouldn't go away, though, so I finally got out of the shower and dried off.

I found myself wanting to talk to Mom and Grandma about the assault. I needed to cry, wanted to cry, and when I cried, I felt better. I knew they could never fully understand how I felt, but they were standing by me and letting me talk and that meant the world to me.

Grandma left that evening, Wednesday, November 29th. I still hadn't slept all afternoon; other than the few minutes I would doze off before having a flashback and waking up once again. Mom hadn't slept either because of the endless phone calls. She said she felt like she never knew what time it was, when she was supposed to sleep or eat or anything. We both agreed that, as far as feelings went, that day ours went into shock.

Mom made out the fold out bed in the living room for me to sleep on. I turned on the television, hoping I could sleep with it on. She said she would be in the next room of I needed her for anything. She kissed me goodnight and went into her bedroom.

I tried to sleep; Lord knows I tried. Each time I fell asleep, I would only awaken from nightmares or some strange noise coming from outside. Mom and Howard had fallen asleep hours ago, but I just could not. I heard the stranger's voice in my dreams, and I woke in the night screaming for Mom. I cried and cried because I wanted to sleep so badly. I was tired and feeling weak from not sleeping.

Mom came running into the living room and I cried, as I felt foolish at needing her to sleep beside me. I felt safe having her there. I felt like I had some protection and I wasn't alone. I felt like I could yell out and someone was there to help me. I was not left alone. I asked her every now and then if she heard any-thing outside. The night was endless, and I could not wait to see the sunlight. I never shut my eyes and it seemed to be an eter-nity before the clock indicated it was time for Mom and Howard to get up for work.

Mom fixed coffee and we smoked a cigarette before she took a shower. I sat in the bathroom with her while she took a shower and we talked. She said I could lay in her bed and watch tele-vision and maybe I would fall asleep. She really didn't want to leave me alone, but she couldn't afford to miss work either.

When it was time for her to go, she turned on the television so I would not be able to hear the noises outside. She had called the landlord and asked him to watch our home because of what happened to me. It was only six-thirty and not many people were up yet, so it was still like night outside. We both looked at the screen and stared. There on the television was the man who had raped me the day before.

The news lady was talking about him being pulled over for a burned-out headlight, when apparently, he took off and started a high-speed chase until the car ran out of gas. Then the news showed my car and the lady went on to say he was a suspect in a rape reported early Wednesday morning. Mom jumped up and down and was saying, "Angie, they got him...they caught him in your car!" I stood there crying and hugging Mom.

Mom called Howard at the grocery store, where they both worked. She told him what we had seen on the television and that she would be a little late. Then she called Grandma and Grandpa. They said they would watch the news at ten and see if it was still on.

I called Dad to let him know and he seemed concerned. He was happy and couldn't believe the guy was stupid enough to be driving around in my car. He told me that if I needed anything at all to call him. He also wanted me to call him when I heard anything new. I felt relieved and happy that he was caught so quickly. Dad told me he loved me and to hang in there and do what I had to do to get the bastard put away. Mom left for work and I started looking for the number to the Broken Arrow Police Department.

Detective Shea had just gotten to the office and had not been to the Tulsa Police Station to talk to the man, who now had a name, William Henry Johnson, Jr. Detective Shea said he would be going over there in a few minutes to get a statement. He asked me if I felt up to coming in the next afternoon to look at pictures and go out to the crime scene. I said that would be okay and asked if he would look for my glasses in the car. I wasn't sure if they were there or not, but it was worth a try because I couldn't see very well without them. He said he would get them if they were there and we hung up.

I called Mom at work and told her what was going on so far and that I had to go and see Detective Shea the following day. She said she would see if Grandma would come down to go with me, in case she couldn't get off work, because I didn't have a car and couldn't see anyway. And I did not want to go alone if we were going to the crime scene because I didn't know how I would react to it.

Grandma came down early in the morning on Friday to go with me to see Detective Shea. Mom didn't think she was going to be able to get off work. Mom left to go to work and then, about fifteen minutes, later called saying they would let her off so she could go with us. Grandma and I waited for Mom to get home before leaving. I was really glad she was able to come because I didn't want to go without her.

When we met Detective Shea, he said he did not recognize me because I looked much better than the last time he had seen me. He gave me my glasses, in a brown paper bag. I pulled them out of the bag and laughed. They were all bent out of shape, and I had to bend them every which way to get them back so that they would fit on my face. I could see again, though, and that was great.

Rick Shea first showed me six photos and asked if I recognized any of the men as being the man who had done these things to me. I really was not sure about any of them, but he said that was all right because the pictures were old. Then he showed me pictures taken off the videotape at the convenient store and I pointed to the man right away. There was no doubt in my mind, that was the stranger, the man I had picked up and the same man I had seen on the channel six news.

After looking at pictures, Detective Shea walked us out to his car. He drove and I sat next to him in the front seat. Mom and Grandma sat in the back seat quietly until we began driving through the neighborhoods.

We drove through all of the neighborhoods, just as I had driven through them on that early morning of November 29th. The night was coming back to me and I was a little discomforted and frightened. I knew I was safe, but I had an eerie feeling and a burning knot in my throat.

Detective Shea began to drive down the road that led to the dead-end. It was not dark now and it was not deserted completely, but it was still scary just the same. When I saw the sign, warning of the dead end, I shifted uneasily in my seat and fought back the tears filling up my eyes. This was the place where it all began. This was where he had begun to beat me. This was where I had felt the first instance of fear and where I had first screamed. This was the place...where I had tried to fight him to get away. It was difficult for me to go back down that road and it was even more difficult to drive down the long, gravel, dirt road leading to the field, thick with foliage, and the quietly flowing river.

When we reached the hidden turn off by the river, where I had been drug to the ground and brutally raped, Detective Shea stopped the car. I got out of the car slowly at first, wondering if my legs were strong enough to carry me. My heart was racing, and I wanted to search that field and to prove to myself that what had taken place there, was real. I wasn't crying anymore, and I was not afraid. I felt ready to look around and to find out what had happened that night.

It didn't look so frightening during the day. It was quiet, and I could see where the police had been because the tall grass was laying down where it had been trampled through. I showed the

Detective where the car had been parked and where Johnson had shoved me to the ground. Then I walked out near the river and showed Detective Shea where I had been abandoned when Johnson had finished beating and raping me. I was a little unsure of the exact location because in the daylight everything looked a little different. But I knew the approximate locations.

Oh, how my emotions were racing. I wanted to keep searching for my shirt, bra, and underclothes, which had never been found. I wanted to find something to tell me why it had happened. I wanted back all the things that belonged to me and that were missing now. Things I would not realize until much later that I would not be able to get back for many, many years. I was searching for an answer to why. Anger was building inside of me that no words could describe. I thought over and over again about how much I wanted that stranger to be put away. William Henry Johnson, Jr. deserved to go away for as many years as possible. Never to hurt another person so long as I was living. Never to see sunlight before my death. I wanted him to pay for what he had taken.

I was quiet on the drive back to the station and on the drive home from Detective Shea's office too. I had many thoughts running endlessly through my mind. I still felt Johnson had some sort of control over me, and that feeling scared me. I feared Johnson night and day and it really did not bring me comfort to know he was in jail.

The next few days spun around in my head. I never had enough time in a day to think about my ordeal. It was at night that I had too much time for my mind to bring forth the absolute horror of my memories. I found myself in tears, asking questions that had no answers. I wanted those answers and needed those answers. I would sometimes dream of the assault only with the outcome in my favor. I would dream of things that I could have done differently.

Each day brought new aches and pains. I could not walk around for two or three days because my ankle and leg would get this sharp pain all the way up into my hip. My ankle wasn't sprained, but it was bruised. My entire face hurt and if I moved my head, even a little, I would get an awful headache. I felt disabled in so many ways. I took pain medications every four hours to keep from feeling anything, because I had pain over every inch of my body.

I was unable to go anywhere because the police were holding my car for evidence purposes. I didn't particularly feel like going anywhere, looking the way I did and not feeling very well, either. I did want to spend some time with Aaron, because I hadn't seen him since the morning at the hospital and I missed him so much. I was feeling very alone when I was unable to be with him. And it did not make me feel any better that he hadn't called me to see how I was or to tell me he was thinking about me.

I talked with Mom about taking me over to his house when she got off work and she said she could drop me off there and pick me up on Sunday if that was ok with Aaron. I called Aaron to let him know I was coming out and to make sure he would be home. He said okay and I was excited about being able to see him after so long. He hadn't even called since the accident, and I was afraid of what he would think when he saw my face.

Mom drove me over to his place on Friday evening, after she had gotten off work and we had eaten dinner. When we arrived at his house, no one was home. All the lights were off, and the cars were gone. Mom and I decided, or rather I begged her, to wait outside for just a while...it turned into an hour. He never came home. We drove back home, and I cried the whole time. I couldn't understand why he wasn't there. He knew I was coming this weekend. Mom said he was no good and I should not be with him because he obviously didn't care about me at all. Moms always see the things we ourselves refuse to see.

I called him all night long and finally reached him around eleven-thirty at night. He did not apologize to me for being so insensitive, he simply said he had been at Michelle's house and they had lost track of time. He had forgotten I was coming out. I told him he could either come out and get me or else I just didn't want to see him for a while. He said he was not coming out so late at night and then he started making me feel that I was the one in the wrong. I hung up with him and felt absolutely terrible.

That was the first time I began to realize that things had changed between Aaron and me. Later, I would learn that he blamed me in many ways, for what I had been through. I was no good to him anymore because I was used. I tried to believe that things were going to be okay with us, but inside it was already becoming clear. I gave him chance after chance to prove he loved me. I spent a weekend with him a few weeks later and he left me at his house all night long, alone. He came home at seven in the morning refusing to talk to me about where he had been but laughing because I was still there.

It was true in my heart what was going on. The heart never lies. I felt the pain already of being forgotten and unloved. I was already left alone, and I knew it. I think I kept hanging on hoping not to feel the inevitable pain and hurt that I knew would come when I had to face the end of our relationship.

Aaron refused to speak about the assault. I was not allowed to talk to his friends about it either. I found that out when I showed the article to one of our mutual friends. Aaron yelled at me and said he didn't think his friends needed to know what had happened. Aaron wanted me to come and visit him, but he also wanted it to be on his terms. I had to stay in his bedroom while he partied with his friends in the living room. He seemed to be ashamed of what I had let happen to me and of the way I looked. I believe he eventually began cheating on me and I just refused to see it. He had gone to someone else for sex or for the love that I was not able to give him. Thing was I think he was looking for a love that was less then I could give him. He was not ready to feel that kind of love for someone and I was. It was a kind of love that went way beyond sex or lust or passion, it came from a deeper place in me.

Everything in my life seemed to be falling to pieces. I felt like I was losing every part of my life. I stopped thinking about

Aaron, at least outwardly. I thought that after I took care of some of my problems, I could work on our relationship. The time apart might be good for the two of us.

The life that I had once led, became only a memory. I couldn't recognize the life I had now. I only thought of the next few months of my life and the many obstacles that lay ahead of me. I spent a lot of time talking with my detective or to Lisa, whose house I had walked to the morning of the incident. I was also at the courthouse talking to the Assistant District Attorney who was prosecuting Johnson. My attorney's name was Eric Stall and my advocate was Elizabeth O'Neal. They were helping me to prepare for the preliminary hearing that would take place in January of 1996.

December of 1995 was a quiet month. Eric had told me that nothing would be happening with the case until after the Christmas holiday, and he was right. I spent December healing, physically, from my injuries. I was able to get my car back from the towing company, only to find I couldn't drive it. Every time I even sat in the car; I would remember what took place the last time I had been in it. I found myself constantly looking around for little things that would let me know that there really was an attack there.

The car still had blood covering the windows and absorbed into the cushions of the seats. Mom and I spent hours shampooing the car, trying to get the blood and the sour smells out. We finally had the car looking better than it ever had did, but it did not make it any easier for me to drive.

December gave me the chance to go and talk to a counselor at Call Rape and to face a few of my fears. I had a wonderful Christmas at my grandparents' house in Bartlesville. It was the most special Christmas I had ever had, and I knew the reason. My family would be together, and I knew just how special each of them was. I had come closer to losing them then I had ever imagined and somehow, I was given a second chance at life. I cried a lot that Christmas, but they were happy tears. Tears of understanding and of thanks. I felt safe and comfortable and warm again.

That was something I had not felt since the rape. I felt peace.

Chapter Four

January 19, 1996 came too soon as far as I was concerned. That was the day of my preliminary hearing and I had prepared myself for that day, with the support and involvement of Elizabeth and Eric, in my case. I knew I could handle the pressures and worries weighing heavily on my shoulders. Eric and Elizabeth had listened as I told and retold the events of that frigid, Wednesday morning. When I felt I could not go through with the trial, they kept me going. When I didn't have any strength left, and I would just break down and cry, they would be my strength. I had made them understand my fears and pains. I had let them feel my sorrow and I knew I could make the judge feel it too.

I woke early on the morning of the nineteenth. I was not excited about going to court, but I realized and was ready to take my first step towards putting Johnson away. I decided to wear a nice pair of jeans and a peach turtleneck, so I would be comfortable and not look too made up. I curled my hair a little and put on a minimal amount of makeup. I looked at myself in my dad's full-length mirror and I felt good about my appearance. Dad had let me sleep in his bed so I could get a good night's sleep since I still was not sleeping through the nights. My stomach was upset, and I was feeling sick, but I knew it was just my nerves. I prayed for everything to go well this day. I would be strong and remember to breathe slowly. I had my whole family supporting me. I would be strong.

I didn't take very many people with me to the hearing. Some of my family had wanted to be there and then decided at the last minute that I might be too uncomfortable having them in the room. Mom, Uncle Tom, Dad and Kim, a friend of Dad's, came to support me. It made me feel good to know that they cared so much and were standing beside me through something so hard to do alone.

When Dad and I arrived at the seventh floor of the courthouse, where the Victim Witness Center was located, I saw Mom, Tom, Linda, from Call Rape, Detective Shea, Elizabeth, and Eric all waiting for me. I said hello and hugged them before finding out what was going on and when we would be going into court.

Eric said it would be about thirty minutes before we would start because other hearings were being set before ours would begin. I talked to Detective Shea while we waited for our turn to go downstairs to the courtroom. Rick Shea had been very compassionate and supportive towards me from the very beginning, and now he had calmed my nerves, so I was feeling much stronger and more positive about the hearing. I knew Detective Shea wanted to see Johnson in prison as much as the rest of us did. He knew, all too well, how much Johnson had hurt me and destroyed my family's lives and mine too. Rick Shea was and would always be a great friend to me, for he played an exceptionally large part in helping me to live again.

I was feeling quite confident and high spirited as I waited, to spite the circumstances. My confidence turned to mush when Elizabeth came in and said it was time. We all went down the elevator together and when we reached the floor of the courtroom and the elevator doors opened, I lost control and began to cry. I couldn't help it, as the tears rolled down my cheeks and I cried openly and freely. Everyone was hugging me and handing me tissue, saying I would do fine. I realized, suddenly, that this would be my first face to face, in the flesh, in the same room, encounter with the man who stole away my life and world.

I had my first perception of what was really taking place. I knew seeing Johnson and having to talk about all the very personal things he had done to me, would be extremely difficult and even embarrassing. It was the fact that, by prosecuting Johnson, I was making sure he could never again hurt any other person, as he had hurt me and my loved ones. I had to do this for all the innocent people who did not deserve to go through what I did or what my family did.

My family had already gone into the courtroom to get seats. I chose to wait out in the hallway until I was asked to take the stand. Detective Shea waited in the hall with me because he was not allowed in during my testimony. Linda waited with us too. They kept me from getting too upset. I thought that was sweet even though nothing could keep me from being upset and nervous and feeling alone. They were wonderful people to even stay out there with me and keep me smiling.

Elizabeth came out of the courtroom and into the hallway where the three of us were waiting. She asked me if I was ready, told me to take a deep breath and handed me some Kleenex. I asked her if Johnson was in the courtroom yet, and she said he was. Elizabeth opened the door to the courtroom and walked in. I walked in behind her and Linda walked in behind me. I felt the tears as they ran down my face. They were hot, burning tears filled full of fear, anxiety, and frustration. I hadn't even seen Johnson, but I could feel him watching me, every step I took. Mom was the first one I saw, then Tom, Dad and Kim. They were all sitting together so that I could look over at them when I felt I might break down or when it got too hard to talk. Dad and Tom were both staring at Johnson and I knew that if they could have, they probably would have gone up and killed that man.

I cried harder still. I suddenly felt very weak and helpless. It was as if, by walking into that courtroom, all the life had drained from my body. So many emotions came raging through me at once and I thought I might faint.

As I was asked questions and giving them answers to those questions. I started to feel very alone. All of the sadness, fear, and anger from within, consumed me. They had merged together, as one, inside of me and I wanted to cry out so badly. It was ripping me apart, feeling as though no one was really hearing me or understanding. I wanted them all to hear about the awful, animal things Johnson had done to me. I wanted to run up to Johnson with that evil, disgusting smile, and I wanted to spit those feelings in his face. I hated him for putting the anger and the hatred that I felt, inside of me. It was a hate that I had never felt towards a human being. Johnson sat there looking so damned nonchalant and comfortable, behind that table. He was so protected, but I didn't have any protection that night when he was ripping every shred of life and love from within me, apart. It seemed as though he was really enjoying the whole ordeal. It seemed to make him feel so powerful to hear about my suffering. It was all so amusing to Johnson, and it made my blood boil and the fire burn deep inside of me more and more with every word I spoke.

I cried through most of my testimony. It was so ridiculously hard to say, in detail, what Johnson had done to me, while my family had to sit there and listen to it. It was not something that you could just close your ears to after all. I wish I didn't have to go into all the details in front of my dad and my uncle, but I had to. I felt so sad and so embarrassed sitting up there. I know it must have been hard on my family. I knew for them to hear those things they had only wondered about before, would bring out a whole different kind of hurt and anger, not to mention a sense of helplessness. To hear the words come from me must have made them see things in a vastly different realization.

I finally felt that I had regained some control from Johnson. I had the power and I was using it to confront the man, who had murdered my spirit, but did not succeed in murdering me. I know that this feeling inside of me was so overwhelming, but I contained it. I wanted so badly to just hurt him as much as I could, but I knew that in time he would pay for what he had done. He had gotten away with rape, there was not a doubt in my mind that society had let this man get away with it. But I was going to make sure that he paid for it with his own life.

Getting through the questions was exceedingly difficult. I tried not to hold it against Mr. Youll, the Public Defender in the case, but I really did have a hard time not wondering how he could ask me these questions and have no remorse or feelings of regret in doing so. I suppose that it is his job and I have no right to judge him for that. After all I did want a fair trial. I did not want to leave any room for appeals.

After being dismissed from the stand, Elizabeth walked me out of the courtroom. Detective Shea was still waiting right outside in the hallway and I walked over and said, "I did it!" Then I hugged him, and I cried so hard. I let it all go and when I had finished, I felt so clean. I felt like I had washed a part of the disgusting and nasty things I had to say in the courtroom, out of me. Linda and Rick and I walked outside to smoke a cigarette and Mom and Tom came out and met us a few minutes later. We all finished our cigarettes and walked back in and took the elevator back to the seventh floor to meet Dad, Kim, and Elizabeth. Dad hugged me and cried. He said he was so proud of me and that I was so strong. I felt weak and I felt good that he thought I was strong and that he was proud of me most of all. I think I had longed for him to be proud of me for years and he finally had said that he was.

I felt I had climbed my first mountain. I hoped that I would be able to move forward, a little, into the real world. Not too far forward, just a few steps, into the world that was filled with unknowing and surprise. Surprises I was not sure I was ready to face.

The judge decided that we had enough evidence to send my case to a jury trial. Johnson's bail had been raised to $252,000 and he would most likely remain in jail until the next trial date. I had won this, my first, fight and now must prepare for my next.

I would be lying to say that even in my preliminary hearing, I did not feel as though I were on trial myself. I did indeed. I felt that I was being looked at and assessed through a microscope even. My every word and gesture being analyzed and dissected to see if there was a hint of dishonesty in them. But though I sometimes felt degraded and dehumanized, I always knew that I was doing something that was not only helping myself, but also helping and seeking justice for all who had been victimized by these violent perpetrators in the past and possibly the future.

Things began to settle down after the preliminary hearing in January. The jury trial would not take place for at least a couple more months and there was a good chance that it would be postponed two or three times. I spent the free time I had, between trials, picking up and trying to put the shattered pieces of my life back together.

I found that I was unable to do so many simple things, everyday things like going to the store or putting gas in the car. Even trips to Wal-Mart were impossible because I always felt like someone was following me. Every man that I saw made me want to hide myself away in a corner somewhere, to hide from the world and make myself invisible.

I hardly ever went out and when I did go out after dark, I was always nervous and reminded of my assault. It was something about the black night and the sense of aloneness that made me feel so unsafe and insecure. I cringed at dead-end signs and my pulse quickened and my heart would jump into my throat. If I had to try and turn around at one of those dead-end roads, I would get sweaty and panicky and feel so faint.

I found so many things hard to do. It often frustrated me that something that was once so easy that I never took the time to think about it, that I did without ever paying the least bit of attention, now seemed to be such a huge obstacle to overcome. I did not understand how the threat of death, by one man, could do so much harm to me. How could he still be controlling my life and still put so much fear into everything I tried to do? I could not understand it. I wanted so badly not to let it affect me or control me, and yet no matter how hard I tried, it was there, taking hold of me and pushing me back against some invisible wall.

Being unable to afford living on my own, without a job, I moved back home with my Dad in January of 1996. I was too afraid to live in Tulsa and I was not safe at my apartment because Johnson knew my address. Mom didn't have the room at her place for me to stay with her and besides Howard felt that Mom was neglecting him a little bit. Dad welcomed me openly and I felt that I would be safer there then I would be anywhere else.

I tried to stay busy and keep my mind off all the negative things that were happening or had been happening to me. I started writing poetry and short stories to pass the time. I tried working, hoping that it might take my mind off of the trial. I really thought that I was ready to work, but I wasn't. I was too afraid and untrusting of everyone at work, to get to know anyone. I ate alone, took breaks alone, had lunches alone. I did everything by myself, becoming silent and withdrawn to real life. I did not care about my own life anymore and so I slipped away into a different life.

I stopped going to work and I stopped living. I could not sleep at night because of the darkness and silence that set in once the sun went down. I began sitting awake all night and sleeping during the day. Every creak or slight sound the house would make, or the animals outside would make, scared me. I only felt safe to sleep when Dad would wake up for work at five in the morning. Sometimes I pretended that I had been asleep just so that no one would ask me. I would even pretend to be going to work or to class in the morning and then come home and sleep after he had left for work. I hated to lie but didn't want anyone to know how hard it was for me, and how I was not sleeping well at all.

I had no control over my own emotions anymore. I often felt desperately alone and frustrated. I felt like I was a small child and my friends and family just could not see or understand how it devastated me. I could not stay alone because I felt so unsafe and vulnerable. It didn't matter where I was, I just knew someone was out there watching me and knew when I was alone. I always locked all the doors and windows and closed the blinds at night. I was obsessed by the thought of someone spying on me or hurting me or invading any part of my private life again.

Aaron and I were not getting along. In fact, I hardly ever saw him or talked to him. I would not accept that Aaron no longer loved me or needed me, even though he had told me on so many occasions. I thought that he was maybe blaming himself or even blaming me for the assault. I loved him and needed him too much to believe that he just did not need me anymore. I knew he thought I was stupid for trying to be nice to a total stranger, especially a man. I knew he probably had feelings of responsibility or blame that he didn't know where to put. I hoped he would understand and in time we could come to terms with the loss we had both been dealt.

We didn't break up during the months between trials, but I could not say we were a couple either. As much as I wanted to believe we were still together, the truth was we were not. We had all but said the words to one another and I wasn't ready to feel the pain of losing him completely. I had the feeling he was cheating on me even though I never actually caught him. My intuition had never led me wrong and I knew it was true, but I didn't want it to be, so I blocked it out. One Sunday afternoon, I went to pick Aaron up to go see a movie and his roommate said he had moved out without notice. I asked where he had moved to, and he said that Aaron had moved into an apartment in Tulsa with two girls, and he thought he was seeing one of them.

I was so shocked and taken aback. Aaron had not even mentioned to me that he was moving, and I had spoken to him just days earlier. I drove home torn between anger and a very deep hurt. I had this sense of abandonment and distrust. I felt betrayed and empty. I called Dad when I got home, and he said he would take off early and come home. That was the day that Dad's hatred for Aaron really began. Dad understood how much I loved Aaron and he didn't like that I was hurting so much.

Our breakup made me feel worse than ever. I needed Aaron to be there and support me and hold me when I was afraid at night. I needed him, not for sex, but for love and understanding and because he made me feel safe. I loved Aaron in a way I could never love another. I did not want to love anyone else in the same way. My love for Aaron was special, and there was no way anyone else could ever have that kind of love from me. When he left, I felt alone and unwanted. I felt used and ugly, and as though I was no longer good enough. The few pieces of my life that I still had seemed to be falling apart as well.

I made myself believe that I had no time for a relationship anyway. I made myself a promise, not to call Aaron until I was over him and had moved on. I also said that I would not see him. Of course, this was really difficult and for the first few weeks I still called him at night and would just lay there with the phone, listening to him breathe and never saying a word. I wanted so badly not to call him though, as it hurt me so much to know he didn't care about me anymore. Eventually, I did not call him, because I knew that if I saw him, or heard his voice, all those feelings I had for him would come back.

I did not date because I was repulsed by the thought of sex or anyone touching me. I felt sick at the thought of anyone, other than Aaron, holding me at night. I knew I was better off alone until I could find myself again. I needed to focus on my upcoming trial, too.

My hearing was set back until May 7th, 1996, as Eric had suspected. We began preparing for the trial in mid-April. We went into greater detail about what had occurred. Eric had me look at maps of the area, in which the rape took place. I was also shown life-size pictures of me right after the rape had taken place. They were photos that had been taken in the hospital during the rape exam.

Eric pulled out about twenty big, brown paper bags containing evidence, such as, the defendants shirt, pants, belt, shoes, my jeans, socks, and afghan Lisa and James had put around me to keep me warm when I had been in their home. All of these things would be shown to the jury, so Eric wanted to make sure I was familiar with them. He also didn't want me to be shocked or upset when the pictures of me came out at the trial.

Eric and Elizabeth told me there would be eleven or twelve witnesses for my case, ranging from doctors and nurses to the highway patrolman who had arrested Johnson. Eric had to offer some sort of plea bargain to Johnson, I guess because that is the way it is done in the court system. But Eric assured me that it would not be to Johnson's liking. Eric felt the case was strong and he really hoped it would go to trial so that everyone could see how nasty a man this William Henry Johnson Jr. was.

I really did not have a clue as to how the court system worked or about plea-bargaining. I wasn't sure plea-bargaining was a good idea because I had heard that it let criminals out in a much shorter time. I wanted Johnson to get as much time as was possible, but I knew he had rights too. He could accept the plea bargain if he wanted to. I personally did not think he should have any rights, but I knew that was something I had to deal with.

Although I was not looking forward to going to trial, I knew it would be my chance to tell Johnson that he not only raped me and left me to die but destroyed the person that I once was. I wanted to let go of all those feelings locked away inside of me. Johnson had taken all that made me who I was. He had stolen those things, in me, that were special and sacred and that no man should ever take away from a woman. He ruined my feelings of the world being honest and trusting. He also stole away my soul and I wanted that back. Only his being in prison would help me to rebuild those things and even then, I knew it would not take away my fears or my memories. I knew I could never be the person I once was.

Chapter Five

May 7th, 1996 came more quickly than I ever imagined it would. I had gone out and bought an outfit to wear to court that day. I chose a pair of slacks and a silk top. I woke up early that morning and ironed my clothes. I took extra care in putting on my make-up and curling my hair, right. I wanted to look respectable for the jury, but even more, I wanted to feel good about myself that day. It was going to be one of the single most important days of my life, and also one of the most unforgettable days.

I already knew what I could expect to hear in court that day because Eric and I had prepared in great length. Eric never lied to me about anything that was going on and he never tried to sugar coat the truth either. I was prepared for the very worst and hoped and prayed for the best. I knew the defense attorney would either try to make me look like a promiscuous whore or say I was accusing the wrong man. I had already been told the stories that Johnson had formulated. One was that I had consented to have sex with Johnson, another was that I had gotten high on marijuana and was masturbating with myself before consenting to have sex with Johnson. There were other variations on the stories too, but I couldn't keep track of them all. He had told so many stories and changed so many details that I couldn't even keep them straight. I was also ready to hear that my boyfriend, not Johnson, had actually raped and beat me, and that I was accusing Johnson to keep my boyfriend out of trouble. The stories were insulting, and demeaning and Johnson must have spent a lot of time cultivating them in jail. I was made aware of them through Eric, so I would not be surprised by anything during the trial. Eric was a very honest and kind man who gave me the respect and understanding I needed.

It made me nauseous every time I started thinking about William Henry Johnson Jr. sitting in his jail cell, plotting, and perfecting his stories and lies. I also thought about the dark grave he was digging himself deeper into every time he thought of another lie to add to one of his stories.

I knew that there was nothing I could say that would be wrong because telling the truth could only be done one way. There are no hidden things, secret paths, or perfected stories in telling the truth. There is simply truth. Johnson had to lie and then come up with more lies to cover the ones he had already told. There was absolutely no way he could remember all those lies, and the pieces just would not fit together to make a believable story. But here I am trying to convince you of this because I am afraid once again that someone won't believe me. Sad how I always feel like I have to prove it. It seemed kind of funny that I had to remind myself that I was not the one on trial. It seemed that my testimony was what would inevitably convince the courtroom of Johnson's guilt or innocence. It was I, who had to prove to the jury that Johnson was the same man who had brutally raped and beaten me. He was, in fact, not a figment of my imagination and I had not consented to having sex, with this stranger. He was the one who had done these inconceivable offenses to me.

I was so ready to cry my eyes out and give them every bloody detail about that night. I needed them to hear me. I needed them to step inside of me and see the damage that Johnson had caused in my life and in my family's lives. I needed them to experience the passion of my words and reach inside and feel my pain. I wanted to bring them into my head and know how it hurt to lose my little sister. I wanted them to know how it felt to have life torn out of my hands and ripped to shreds. To look outside of myself and see that all of my life had been scattered around me.

Even more than that, I wanted Johnson to pay for the rest of his life, for the few hours of power and control he got on November 29, 1995. I wanted to walk into that courtroom with my head held high and show Johnson what control really was. I wanted to go in there and take back my life.

That Tuesday morning, I could not eat breakfast. I felt as nauseated as I had the morning of the preliminary hearing back in January. I was extremely apprehensive and disturbed, but I kept telling myself that I was going to be fine. I tried singing to myself to keep the trial out of my mind. I, momentarily, was not sure what to expect from the day ahead of me. I focused on staying calm, not getting too eager, and trying to smile despite the awful circumstances of the whole day. Dad knew I was nervous and was trying to make me feel better by telling me to just go out there and answer the questions they asked, the best that I could and put that man away.

Dad and I left the house just after seven in the morning. We dropped Shauna off at daycare and then left for Tulsa. Dad stopped at QuikTrip and we got donuts and something to drink. Then we went by April's house before going to the courthouse. April only lived a couple blocks from the courthouse so I told her we could pick her up on our way there.

The rest of my family would be meeting us at the courthouse because they were all riding in together. Mom, Uncle Tom, Grandma and Grandpa, and Kim were all coming. Detective Shea and Lisa Frederick would be there, as well as Jacque, a friend since grade school.

When we arrived at the Victim Witness Center, on the seventh floor of the courthouse building, everyone was waiting on me. Elizabeth and Eric asked the family to come into the meeting area that had glass enclosing it and separating it from the waiting area. Dad hadn't made it up yet because he was still parking the car. Parking at courthouses was almost impossible and we were going to be there all afternoon, so it took a while to find a place.

I wanted to wait for Dad before Eric began explaining what was going on. Dad got there a few minutes later and Eric began. He explained what had taken place the day before. They had selected a jury of twelve and one alternate. Eric said that Johnson had gotten angry, saying he was not being accurately represented, and dismissed his attorney, David Youll. Johnson said he wanted to represent himself in court. Johnson had then changed his mind, calling his attorney earlier in the morning, and asking David Youll to represent him once again. Johnson had also decided to plead guilty to the charges brought against him.

Eric explained that he had offered a plea bargain, as is required. The plea bargain was for Life plus Forty-five years. He had offered this to Johnson and his attorney, and if it were accepted then we would go before the judge. Judge Hopper then had to accept Johnson's plea of guilty as being honest and truthful, as well as reasonable. Basically, it meant that the judge had to be sure Johnson wasn't coerced into his decision by anyone. If everything went well, I might not have to testify at all. Eric assured all of us that the amount of time he was offering to Johnson was a good chunk of time and I should feel good about that.

Despite everyone telling me that I shouldn't get my hopes up just yet, because there was still that possibility that we would have to go ahead with the trial, I was delighted. I mean I was anxious and nervous inside and just wanted to hug everyone and be happy. I felt relieved just knowing that Johnson was obviously not so sure about his fate, anymore.

Eric left us, to go downstairs to the courtroom and see how everything was coming along. I started looking around the waiting area for Lisa. I finally spotted her reading a magazine, so I walked over and said hello. I hardly recognized her because her hair was curled, and she was dressed up for the trial.

I filled her in on what Eric had just told us and then I introduced her to my family. She and Mom had already met at Christmas, when Mom and I took her and her family a plant, as a thank-you for helping me. Lisa had never met the rest of my family though, and I knew Dad really wanted to meet her and thank her for everything she had done for me. Lisa and her family had, after all, saved my life. We all sat outside the Victim Witness

Center, on the benches running along the wall, so we could all sit and talk together. We waited all morning and Elizabeth and Eric would occasionally come and let us know if it was getting any closer to time for us to go in. We waited until noon, and then Elizabeth came over and said everyone was breaking for lunch. She said our case would be the first one after lunch, so we needed to back at ten minutes before one. Everyone was hungry so we tried to decide where we could go eat that wasn't too far away.

We finally decided on a place called "Interurban". Lisa, Kim, Dad, and I rode in one car and everyone else took another car. Detective Shea sort of disappeared to his own favorite eating-place. We all took the time to relax and talk about the trial, while we ate. The hour went by very quickly and before long it was time for us to get back to the courthouse. My palms were already sweaty and the food I had just eaten was aggravating my stomach. I had already begun to get nervous and I hoped and prayed God would let everything work out all right.

We had barely stepped out of the elevator onto the seventh floor, when Elizabeth said they were ready for us to go down to the courtroom. I was afraid Dad wouldn't know where to find us because he was out trying to park the car again. I took a deep breath as we all took the elevator downstairs. I was trying my hardest not to cry, but I did anyway. I was used to the tears by then, so I just let it go. Everyone was hugging me and reassuring me that everything would be fine. I began to feel a little stronger with everyone encouraging me.

It felt good to have so many supportive family and friends with me. I expected Johnson to already be in the courtroom when I walked through the big, wooden doors, but he had not been brought in yet. I sat beside Lisa, on the front row, and Mom, April, Tom, Grandma and Grandpa, and Jacque sat on the rest of the row. Kim and Elizabeth sat behind me and held a place for Dad, who hadn't made it back yet. I hoped he would make it before they brought Johnson in, because I really needed him there. Dad walked in, thank God, and I sighed in relief. Detective Shea stood at the back of the room with the highway patrolman who had arrested Johnson.

William Henry Johnson, Jr. had not come through those doors yet, and neither had his public defender, David Youll. Elizabeth said she would tell me before he came in and she handed me some Kleenex. I looked around the room and noticed only a few people sitting on the other side of the courtroom. I figured they were probably from the newspaper. I wondered secretly if any of them were friends or family of the stranger.

I could not help but keep staring towards the door. I tried not to look but I knew any moment Johnson would be walking through it. I wondered if he would be in handcuffs or if he would be free. Elizabeth came over and said Johnson was getting ready to come in, so I quickly passed the message along to everyone else. Eric came over and asked if I was ready and said that everything would be fine. I held my breath, said a silent prayer, and squeezed Lisa's hand. I wondered if she was uncomfortable about seeing Johnson for the first time.

The doors opened and Johnson walked into the courtroom without handcuffs. He was wearing a button-up shirt, that he hadn't bothered to tuck in, and a pair of faded, black jeans. David Youll walked in behind Johnson, but I hardly noticed. I kept thinking that Johnson would run over and try to hit me again. He walked not more than two feet away from me. I could have stood up and slapped him. I lost control and started crying again. I could not see for the tears that blurred my vision. I squeezed Lisa and Dad's hands like I was holding on for my life. Dad whispered in my ear, "It's okay" and I could hear the emotions he was trying to hold back.

I searched Johnson from head to toe, looking for a sign of the violent stranger that I had remembered him to be. I searched his face, his hands, his fingers, his legs and even his feet. The horror of it all was he looked so nice and normal. I saw nothing of the violent man I had seen before. He seemed so innocent, just as he had seemed when I first met him, back in November. But his hands, they were so big and rough looking. I saw those hands hitting and beating on me. It was his hands that told me this was the same man who had hurt me months earlier.

Lisa squeezed my hand bringing me back from the memories that had begun to consume my thoughts. She had not realized that Johnson was a black man and it took her by surprise. I had forgotten that she had not seen him before this moment and that I never mentioned what color his skin was. I guess because it wasn't the color of his skin that hurt me or made him do what he did, it was what was locked inside of the man, that hurt me and made me fear him.

Everyone was asked to rise as Judge Hopper entered the courtroom. We were seated and the trial began. The way Judge Hopper started made me think we were going to go ahead with a jury trial, but David Youll stepped in after a couple minutes. He told the judge that the defendant, Mr. Johnson, wished to take back his plea of not guilty and enter a plea of guilty. Judge Hopper asked that Johnson and his defender, David Youll, come forward, then he asked Eric to approach the bench as well.

I cried throughout the time that Johnson was explaining the details of what he had done to me. I could see, so clearly, every moment of the assault, as it played like a movie, in my mind. I heard Dad crying behind me and he squeezed my hand. I knew how hard it must have been for him to hear about all the disgusting things Johnson had done. It was harder still to hear it from the mouth of the man who had done them. Lisa was crying, too, and I felt that all of us were brave and strong and helping each other through that day.

Eric would look over and smile every once in a while, just so I would know everything was going well. He even walked over and squeezed my hand and whispered something to reassure me. It was difficult to sit quietly and listen to Johnson, as he spoke of what had happened. I never heard the slightest sound of regret in his voice. I heard no feelings or emotions of any kind in Johnson's words.

William Henry Johnson, Jr. did ask Judge Hopper if he could

have the chance to apologize. That was the only time I ever thought maybe Johnson was being truthful or sincere. His apology only made my insides hurt more. I had asked myself for more than five months, why it had to happen, and why it had to be me. I could not find it in my heart to forgive that man. He had completely destroyed my life and the lives of everyone I loved. I felt that he was using his sweet, charming, innocent voice to make us all believe him. Johnson said that he had turned toward the Lord or found God while in jail, and I truly hoped that he had. I just could not find a way to forgive him, and it hurt me to feel like that because I had always been the first to forgive anyone. He had changed that in me.

Judge Hopper accepted Johnson's plea of guilty and made certain that Johnson understood the rights he was giving up in pleading guilty. The judge then read off the list of charges brought against Johnson and the amount of time for each charge. Johnson was sentenced and immediately sent from the courtroom.

Once Johnson had been taken away in handcuffs, I felt an enormous weight had been lifted from me. Elizabeth came over and said I could go out and smoke a cigarette, if I wanted to, or I could stay and see the jury. Judge Hopper had to bring them in and explain to them that Johnson had decided to plead guilty. I really needed a cigarette, so Lisa, Jacque, Kim, and I went outside. The others wanted to stay and see the jurors.

We smoked our cigarettes and talked for a few minutes, trying to calm down because our adrenaline was so high. We took the elevators to the seventh floor where we were meeting the others. Eric, and everyone else who had been there for the trial, was waiting when we made it up the stairs. I hugged Eric, Detective Shea, Elizabeth, and everyone else who had supported me. We all said how happy we were that it was finally over.

I felt as though a chapter in a book had just closed. Everyone went down in the elevator together and hugged once again before going our separate ways. Tears began to fill my eyes as I thought about the new family, I had gained during the last several months. It was sad to say good-bye, knowing I would probably never see them again. They had become an important part of my life and I wasn't ready to let go of that yet. Eric gave me the huge pictures of myself that we were going to use in court, so I could keep them. They would come in handy when Johnson came up for parole. He said he hoped he never saw me again under the same circumstances and we said good-bye. That would be the last time I ever saw Eric, Detective Shea, or Elizabeth.

Dad, Kim, and I went for drinks after court and then eventually we made our way home. Actually, I shouldn't even lie about it, but I am so used to keeping the secret that I always lie. Dad had to stop at his friend's house and get some drugs before we went home. He was feeling good and we were both a little drunk, but he wanted to see his friend and tell him about it. I got to watch him do drugs and then I drove us home. I called Mom and went over to visit her. I felt bad because I had ignored her that afternoon. I felt that I had not paid any attention to her and it was mean, and I was feeling really down about it. I spent a long time with Mom that night and I hope she knows I was there because I love her. One chapter had closed, but I knew there were many more just opening up.

Chapter Six

I thought that by getting Johnson sent to prison, my life would begin to piece itself back together. I thought I would feel as I felt before the assault. I found that I had thought wrong. My fears, memories and emotions were still very apparent and extraordinarily strong, and I had so much that I was unable to deal with. Things I just didn't know how to talk about or think about or forget.

The nightmares eventually faded away, occurring only occasionally, but the nights were still endless all the same. I couldn't call whatever it was keeping me awake at night, nightmares, but rather illusions or hallucinations. It was as if the stranger was really there. I would wake in the night to find this perfect image of Johnson, standing so still before me, just staring. He always stood beside my bed and I felt as though I could reach out and touch him. I realized he was not really there, but it did not keep me from seeing him there all the same. I assumed I would probably always have those illusions and I would somehow have to deal with them, as well as the flashbacks and memories.

I decided to enroll in summer school classes in June of 1996. I hadn't graduated from high school and I wanted to go back and get my diploma. I enjoyed the English and art classes that I was taking. They kept me busy for a while and I graduated at the end of June with A's. I felt really good at having accomplished something I had wanted for a long time.

I tried working but was never happy. I didn't feel like going to a job that I hated. I only worked because Dad said I had to if I wanted to keep living at home. I was not motivated or interest in anything. I wanted to close myself off from the world because I did not feel I belonged anywhere.

The months slowly came and went, and I cut myself off from society more and more. I was not the girl that I once was, and I knew deep inside that I never could be. The trauma of the rape was becoming very apparent. Realizing that it was I, who had been raped, was difficult. I still could not believe it really happened to me. I could not understand it and I could not answer any of my questions. It was only because I was feeling the depression and desertion inside of myself that I had to begin facing that what had happened was not my imagination. It did, in fact, take place. It hit me awfully hard and I found it difficult to deal with.

Everyone around me expected me to move forward with my life, yet, I felt as though I was in neutral. I wondered if I was normal to feel as I did. My life revolved around a central power and that was "the rape".

I wanted to hear someone say that it was okay for me to feel isolated and to dwell on my attack, as I was. I thought about it almost every second of every, single day. I felt I was almost obsessed with it.

My friend moved back from Texas before the trial and she had been supportive during the trial and even for a while afterwards. Things began to change though. She continuously argued with me about what I should have done. Once she told me I should have fought harder and never stopped fighting him. Fight harder! I was so humiliated by her words or that she could even say something so cruel to me, that I felt like crying. She had not been there, and I did not feel like she had the right to tell me that what I had done or had not done that night, was wrong.

I was told, during a conversation I had with a friend's mother, that robbing a person was just as bad as raping them. I could not understand how that could be even remotely close to raping someone. The only thing I could say about that conversation was that I would much rather have someone steal my jewelry, money, or car then to steal my body and soul.

I had no choice but to hear things that made me feel so guilty and ashamed. Although, I knew in my heart that I had done nothing wrong, I found myself constantly fighting back against the allegations to defend my self-worth. I often felt that my friends put me on trial more than when I was actually going to court.

One friend was giving me some of his advice on what to do if something like that ever did happen again. He said that I should pretend to enjoy it and then bite the man's balls until the guy was bleeding. When I responded with anger and said that I would never get that close and if I were ever forced to, I would probably be too scared that the man would kill me to actually go through with it. My friend told me that he would have no sympathy for me if it happened again, because next time it would be my own fault since he had just given me this advice.

Sometimes people are very hurtful, whether they do it intentionally or not, they will do it. Rape made me an outcast in so many ways. It also made me extremely sensitive towards many situations. I saw situations throughout my everyday life that troubled me, such as young girls who believed sleeping around was just a game, or girls who would go out drinking and getting high, because that was supposed to be cool. Those girls put themselves in situations that were dangerous without realizing what consequences they could be facing, even though it is never your fault when you are raped.

I could no longer listen to rap music because the lyrics were so tasteless. The artists seemed to promote violence and rape and make their listeners believe it was not a dominant act. I also noticed how many sexual comments that were degrading towards women, were made every day.

I dealt with issues that seemed so trivial to me before the assault. These were issues that affected me in an entirely changed way after my incident. I did not know sometimes why I was fanatical about my beliefs, but I was struggling to find an identity I could call my own and my beliefs were the one thing I had.

In July of 1996, I went to a gynecologist to make sure that everything was okay. I thought I might possibly have had hemorrhoids because I was bleeding and very sore. I was also worried because I had no periods in almost three months. I found out, shortly after seeing the doctor, that I had contracted venereal warts from Johnson and that news upset me a lot. It was just another setback in my recovery, and I had already had too many of those. I would need surgery to remove them and that was not something I needed or wanted to deal with at that time.

I still could not find the courage to date or even begin to have a close relationship. The thought of being touched by any man made me sick inside. I did not even want a man to tell me that I was beautiful, much less that he loved me.

I had settled into a severe depression and my days were filled with uncontrollable crying and endless thoughts of suicide. They were thoughts that I could not go through with, but I was dealing with some profoundly serious and very scary issues. As I saw it, my life had disappeared and there was no reason for me to try and regain control anymore.

I celebrated my twenty-first birthday on October 30th, 1996. I was considered a legal adult and yet I had regressed in my own life, to an incompetent child. The nights had begun to grow colder and there was an unmistakable chill in the air. The ground had covered itself in a blanket of frost and felt icy beneath my feet. It brought me to remember that night almost a year before.

Life continued to be unchanging for me. The harder I searched life and dissected it, the more I wished I could be someplace else. I had what I called "near break downs" where I would just lie in my bed and pretend the whole world just did not exist. Sometimes, I wanted to commit myself to a hospital for treatment and counseling. I still do not understand why sometimes I cry, or why I feel so alone sometimes. I cannot explain the empty space that is inside of me and consumes my life. It holds nothing and accepts nothing, and it grows bigger and bigger each day.

I suppose that it isn't possible for me to change the past and I can never hope to forget that night I lost myself. The time Johnson spends in prison cannot erase the scars that I will carry with me for the rest of my days. It will never right the wrong he did to me or to my family, nor could it ever make the passing of one more year any easier.

There are only a very few things we must deal with alone, in our lives. This is one of those few things I must go through on my own. One day, I hope to be able to open my door and feel free and safe. Then I might be able to live once again.

Maybe it is knowing that something is hurting inside of me that I cannot get to go away, that makes it such a blow to life for me. The true and raw horror of rape is not the violence of the beating, or even the forced and prohibitive sex. The horror lies much deeper and once it has been burned into your soul, it cannot be shaken away or disregarded. It is the stealing of the soul, of one's own identity, that is irreplaceable. It is the loss of life that has brought about my dejection.

What I still remember, today, is the predominant fear of dying. I had to say good-bye to those that I loved, and I wasn't ready to do that, because I was not ready to die. I was afraid that little Shauna would not remember me, except for a few, fading memories and pictures. How could I die without holding her little hand and telling her how very much I loved her? How could I do that?

I was simply being nice to a man that seemed to need help. I was not looking to die, not like that and not that night. Most of the questions that lingered in my head had no answers and I still do not have answers. No one can explain what that man was thinking that could possess him to something so immoral. I must accept that and try not to question it.

Rape had always been a foreign word to me. Sure, I knew what rape was, but I never though in a million years that it could happen to me. I had read so many times about other people, people I did not know, being raped. I saw stories on the news and felt terrible for those people, but I just never believed it could happen to anyone that I knew and especially not to me. I used to think that if I ever did get into a situation such as that, I could defend myself. I had this huge misconception about what

I could and could not do in that situation. All that I know is that if it had not been me walking into that store, it would have been some other innocent victim. Because I do not believe I am the only kind person in this world, and I do not believe any of us are immune to the dangers.

I know someday these memories will fade to a place somewhere deep within me. I know, too, that I will once again trust people. I will one day love again and be able to enjoy the closeness of a relationship. For the moment, I can only slowly rebuild my self-esteem, my dreams, and my strength. Slowly, I will make this life mine once again. Until that day finds me, I can rest assured that William Henry Johnson, Jr., the stranger, the evil man, will spend the next twenty-five years or more, in prison.

Johnson took my life from me and so I took his in return. May God reach him and change his heart and take away that man's anger and fear. Still, he got away with rape and much more. I feel lost.

Chapter Seven

I was often asked if I was given some sort of sign or premonition, that something was not right, before the assault actually happened. That question is exceedingly difficult to answer because people tend to think that I could have somehow prevented what happened from happening. It is also difficult to answer simply because I was giving a ride to a person whom I had never met before. It was completely normal to feel some sense of discomfort in that situation. Yes, I did feel a bit uneasy, but I figured it was justified given the circumstances.

Johnson and I did make small talk about rather unimportant things, during the drive. I drove around for nearly an hour, so it was natural that we talked some. He gave me the impression of being a man who had been through a rather upsetting ordeal, but he did not present himself as rude or unpleasant, and definitely not as a threat.

I really felt that everything was okay. I admit that I was frustrated about having to drive for such a long period of time, and many searching thoughts went through my mind, but I wanted to do something nice for someone else. Many individuals have told me that that is where I made my mistake. I began to get susceptible and I let my vulnerability show. The only advice I feel I can give to others is that no one looks like a rapist, or any other type of criminal. No one can be trusted by how charming that they act or well-dressed they may be. Rapists come in all shapes and sizes, races, backgrounds, and genders. They cannot be picked out of a crowd.

To date, I suspect everyone that I meet until they show me, they can be trusted and that I can believe in them. I, sometimes, hate that I cannot have the same trust in society that I once had. I do not trust friends, co-workers, and even some family. I realize that I am never going to be one hundred percent safe. I have learned in an extremely hard way, from what I have gone through. I also know that even with the knowledge that I have gained, I still have as great a chance as the next person of being raped again.

I have asked myself questions since the night of my assault that I could not answer. Questions about why men rape and what triggers their minds and forces them to commit such brutal crimes. In the process of writing my story, I read many books on rape and sexual violence, and I learned some important facts and received some interesting answers to my questions.

There is not a definite, distinct motive that could answer the questions as to why men rape. It may be opportunity, or possibly emotional illness, lust or maybe it is not any of these reasons. Anger...a deep, foreboding, and mysterious anger seems to be the most common thread among men who choose to rape. And I might add that it is a choice.

Victims, such as I, are simply objects in their attacker's eyes. Rapists do not see us as having a mind or a heart. I believe rapists are on some sort of power trip, choosing a vulnerable female who is half their size and punching, choking, and kicking her into submission. It is the attacker's way of degrading his victim because sex is in so many ways considered dirty or sinful. This is why rape is the single worst thing a rapist could do to his victim.

Someone once told me that rapists do not get pleasure out of raping. I think that the very thought, of forcing sex on an individual and controlling them, excites a rapist in such a way that ordinary and consensual sex does not. It is the sense of such great power, control and dominance that excites them and drives them.

I have found myself on a roller coaster of emotional highs and lows. People who are close to me think that just because it has been a year since the assault that I should be okay now. They cannot see the hurt anymore, so it must not exist. The bruises have gone away, but the scars are still there, and I still hurt. People would say to me, "Angie, you are such a strong person", but I did not want to be seen as Superwoman. I wanted to be looked after. I had to pretend to be strong out of self-respect, but I wanted someone to see that I was not strong at all.

Images and memories continuously plague my mind and spirit. I am fighting against myself. I fight every day against my low self-image, and my anger about the rape. I fight my fears and my weaknesses. I feel that I cannot stand up for myself anymore because I am not sure whom I am defending. Often, I don't even care what happens to me.

I felt incapable, confused and a failure. The sight of my own body disgusts me. I look into the mirror and I hate what I see. I want to be with a man in a normal way again, but I cannot. Johnson did all this to me.

I haven't got the patience or tolerance with myself that I once had. I know people are talking about me and thinking, "Why aren't you better yet?" and I feel that way too. Why am I not better yet? I feel devastated both emotionally and sexually by the assault. I find that all I can do is have faith in my own strength.

I have always felt that my family suffered as much, if not more, than I did, over the rape. I find myself still shielding my thoughts from them because I am not sure that they are ready or able to cope with my feelings. I would very much like for my family to talk to me and share, with me, their reactions to my rape, and to share their own worries and fears.

I believe that each and every victim and survivor has her own special gift for facing a crisis. I know that once I was able to confront my rape and see it for what it was, I realized that it could not be undone and I was slowly able to start making positive changes in my life. First, I had to look at my fears and face them, rather than denying them.

The deepest horror of being raped, for me, lies in the fear of being killed. The terror of being murdered is the most traumatic measure of rape, and yet it seems to be the most overlooked. I came face to face with my own death and it will take a lot of time to recover from that. I felt a complete separation of my mind and body, as if the rape were happening to someone else. It seemed as if time stood still and nothing was real anymore.

Rape is not about sex and anyone who has been a victim could tell you that. Rape is solely about violence and violation. People forget that rape is an assault, not sex. Weapons come in many different forms, including fists, strength, height, weight, and threats.

Since writing this book I have decided to add a couple of things to it. I thought I should be honest with my readers, as they would expect me to be. I have hard times. I have extremely hard times and I will not pretend to have recovered from this even though at this point it has been more than four years since the rape.

Still, no one understands why it is still part of me, and why this tragic assault has taken so much from me. I do not have an answer for it. I wish I could tell all the survivors who are just beginning the process of recovery, that there is a really happy ending here, but it's real life. I am alive and I am dealing, and I am laughing more. I have made some changes in my life, and I have found myself, but it is still hard. I won't lie and say that I never think about the rape because I do. I think about it every day. But the good news is that it does not keep me up all night long anymore. I don't have nightmares about the stranger.

After the Rape

The letters below were written after the assault. I went through so many hard times when I was searching for myself. It took me about a year to get off the streets. I am now much more than I ever believed I would be. I knew my dream was there somewhere, I just had to find it and believe enough in myself, to reach out for it. Here is a letter I wrote, not meant for anyone, but to make me feel a little better during a difficult time. I also wrote a letter to the stranger who raped me to let go of so much of the anger and frustration that I was holding inside.

Letter One

I don't really know if I can blame the events of my life, since the rape, on the rape itself, or not. In many ways I feel I can blame the rapist, Johnson, but in other ways it does not seem logical, since he has spent the past months in prison.

All that I can say honestly is whomever is to blame, probably myself, has done a wonderful job of making my life a living hell every single day. I do not know where I am living from day to day. I sometimes drive around for hours in my car with no real place to go. Other times I might just sit in a parking lot or a park, wishing I might possibly be able to sleep for just a couple of hours, somewhere.

Keeping a job seems to be unmanageable. Finding different places to work is not hard at all. There are so many jobs out there, and it is easy to hide all the sleepless nights and hunger pangs beneath a less than perfect smile.

Between the sickness of being a "brittle" diabetic, which is just a cop out meaning I either do not want to accept that I am diabetic, or that I don't know how to control it. I tend to believe that it's more likely the latter. Either way, between my diabetic control problems and my depressive thoughts of being homeless, overweight, hungry, suicidal, and fearing a breakdown, I cannot seem to keep a job.

It's hard to explain and most people simply call it laziness, but I know it's not. Have you ever wondered why a homeless person does not work? Well, some do I suppose, though I have never met one who did. But my point is that those who are less fortunate and end up couch surfing, living in their cars, or under bridges, etc... cannot bathe, wash their hair, brush their teeth, wash clothes, and put on make-up. These things are sort of important, and though for a while they can manage to look presentable and hide the circumstances by which they live, after showing up to work with the same pair of pants or body odor reeking from them, someone will surely notice and they most likely will be fired.

There are many trials laid upon each of us throughout our lives. I try to see the future and how everything will surely piece itself together one day. I see myself in college, with a cozy little apartment, maybe a boyfriend. I see these things but there is a wall between my dreams and myself. This wall that does not seem to want to give.

Tomorrow, I will probably go to a shelter. Not a shelter for battered women or for runaways, but a homeless shelter. You see, I haven't got a home to go to, a bed to sleep in, or a shower to wash. I haven't got a job to look forward to or food to keep me healthy. This is why my hope is gone. It is only by faith that I am here at all instead of dead.

Believe me, thoughts of suicide are as common to me as anything else thought about from day to day. But I realize one day I will be more than I am today.

To die now would be too easy. To die now, no one would really care. In fact, my death would make a lot of people's lives a whole lot easier. No more worrying for my mom and for my sister. No more being accused of stealing, lying, cheating for me. But wouldn't that be too easy? I think so.

I never know what each day will bring. I like the daytime. I can walk in the park or go and write. I never eat unless someone can give me free food. I worry about where I will sleep at night and if I will sleep at all.

Nobody wants to help me anymore. No one wants to have to worry about me anymore. They have friends, jobs, homes, and lives of their own. Angie is not important to them.

I know they will be there when I have my own place, my own money, and my own life. But I will always remember how they turned away from me and turned me away.

Letter to Stranger

I have so many questions that I have no answers for. I have so many things that I want to say and do not know how to say them. I do not understand how you could do what you did, to me. Why did you do it? I was only helping you, and you hurt me. You hurt me!!!!

You dominated me, screamed at me, beat me, raped me. You did not hear me screaming and pleading for you to stop. You just went on and on, as if seeing me bleed and cry and hurt was something enjoyable or fascinating for you.

Do you know that I cannot date? Still, after three years, I remain alone. I have had to rebuild every part of my life and myself from the ground up. I had to find self-worth and respect for myself because you took it from me. I could not sleep at night or be alone for fear you would be there. I was living the life of a small child all over again. I didn't have control over anything, and it was you who caused these things.

I no longer have the love of my life, or the life I once had. I no longer have the same trust for this place I live in. I used to be proud that I was able to give others my trust and friendship so easily, knowing they would never take advantage of it. I believed in people. You took that away from me, you stole that.

You stole my gift of love and the special feelings that affix to that gift. You stole my life away from me and I cannot understand why. Maybe you don't even realize how life changing what you have done, has been for me.

What makes you think that you can just take anything that you want, or that my life and my dreams were yours to destroy? Who are you to play God with my life? How could you put such a fear...such a fear of death into me? How could you take this life of a young twenty-year-old girl? Who gave you the right to demote me to a level of self-worth that you found appropriate?

You are nothing!! Do you understand these words? Do you understand what I am telling you? You should have had your dick cut off and your head kicked in continually. You should be violated in such an inhumane way. You should be the one left naked and bloody and cold in the dead of winter, to die alone. You should feel like nothing but waste and never be allowed to have your life back. This is what you deserve because of the small, pathetic, bastard of a man that you have proven yourself to be. No matter how much repentance you do in prison and how many times you say you are sorry, you will always be the same loser to me.

You had to act out your own personal indignation and disappointment, by destroying an innocent individual and savoring every single moment, as you thrashed, kicked, lacerated, spit, cussed and raped me. You are a pig and whether you truly have found God or you were simply using that pleasant, compassionate voice you have used so many times before, and use so well, you will still spend the rest of this life in hell. I will make sure of this as long as I am living and breathing, and I AM living. You will never see beyond the bars you are now dying behind.

I am so angry!! I will not let you control my life from the prison that you rot in. You think every day about the sick and twisted mind you have and the brutal and pathetic person you have shown yourself to be.

I heard you say how deeply sorry you were, but those words don't mean a thing to me. They mean absolutely nothing, because I trusted you to be a man who needed some help because you were having a bad night. You turned out to be a liar, a con. You are abusive and you are toxic. You are only concerned with where you can get your next fix and whom the next poor woman will be that you can beat on. God forbid if I had let you get away with that and hurt some other innocent person.

Next time you decide to do such a stupid and destructive crime, you should think twice. Of course, I have seen to it that you never get that chance again. You are so welcome! It was the best thing and the most gratifying thing I have ever been able to do. You do not deserve love, life, or children. Enjoy your loneliness and drown in my blood, tears, wounds, and most of all my soul.

It does not even matter, anymore, why you did it or if you are sorry for it. You did it and you cannot take it back. It takes a very evil man to do something like what you have done. It takes a ridiculously small man to laugh in the face of someone who is in such pain. You sucked so much life from me and you still could never understand. I do not even want you to understand.

You know nothing about me. You thought I was weak and would never go through with the trial. I could never have turned my back on something that would put you away for life. Just think of all the things you are missing out on. You will never be a part of your son's life; you will never know true love again. You can swallow your pride now because no one thinks you are cool anymore. You are a bastard.

You have nothing to offer the world. You are the perfect example of a violent, dirty, wretched man. I know that it is wrong for me to feel like this, but I have the right. I should be forgiving, but why? You were not compassionate when I hurt. You did not hear me when I cried. You think I am not human because some woman hurt you, and you were angry? That is no excuse. God forbid, a woman hurt you. Do you think you are the only one who has ever been hurt? Wake up asshole.

I hope that your home in prison is as cold and heartless as you were. I am alive. I have clean air to breathe and many new experiences to find. I have so much life left in me. You did not break me. I had to do some adjusting and I have lifelong changes to make, but I have won this fight. In the end, I guess all that power you tried to show everyone kicked you in the ass. God bless you and I hope one day before you die, you truly pray for forgiveness, not from me, but from God.

The Spirit You Murdered

This Is My Life

Coma

I was raped in 1995, 25 years ago. So many changes came from such a horrible tragedy. Sometimes I still can't see it clearly, as though maybe if I don't recognize it then it isn't there. But it is. I find it hard somehow to explain why I am glad for what it did to me, but I feel like I should explain it. I was weak, vulnerable, and naïve. I believed in people and I trusted my country and my world. You might say that I felt invincible to evil. Much like many people think. If anyone tried to hurt me, I could get out of it. I would fight them off and I would win. I thought I knew. I thought that I was smarter than that, but the truth is I wasn't.

I don't want to go too much into my rape because I have an entire book committed to that. What I do want to share is that, the rape changed me, the trial changed me, the struggle to feel normal again and not be embarrassed by what had happened had changed me.

After my rape, I felt like there was no soul inside of me. I felt like every good thing about me had been stolen away and all that was left was ugliness and death. My world was not the same as I remembered it. I was numbed by what I had seen and what I had felt. Numbed by the pure evil that one man possessed. A child in a 20-year-old body. I didn't know how to be with people, didn't know how to love or to laugh or to talk. I didn't know how to trust in anything.

After my rape, the trial, and months of reliving it over and over in my mind, friends and family thought I would move on. In fact, I did just the opposite. I slept days instead of nights somehow thinking it was safer, more secure if I slept during daylight hours. The first part of this book was written during the long, sleepless nights I had made a routine. As the world slept, I wrote. Sometime in 1997 my Grampy died, and I moved to Afton, OK to live with my Gran-Gran, not sure if it was so I could help her to live without him, or if it might have been so I could run away. In any case, I moved to this small, country town with very little to do other than play bingo on Friday & Saturday nights.

My loneliness took control and I died inside the prison that I had built myself. A prison that I thought would keep me safe from my life. I was wrong. I hurt so much that I stopped taking my insulin and I began to eat all the time to blanket my pain and give me the only comfort I could embrace. I just kind of gave up, to put it simply. I was not excited about anything or by anyone. Moving to Grove, Oklahoma was the worst decision I could have made for myself. I had moved there because I felt like I caused my family a lot of pain. I had bad luck and I was more of a burden than an asset to my family.

I acquired a job in Grove, OK about 10 minutes from my grandma's home, at a local resort & golf club called Shangri-la. It was a really nice place and I was a bartender making drinks behind the scenes for the restaurant. But I was very unhappy. Away from my family, my Mom, my sisters, my boyfriend, my friends left me so isolated that I spent most of my time with my cousin, Shelle, and her friends. I don't want to speak badly of anyone but things her and her friends and her mother did just didn't sit well with the values and the upbringing I had been so used to. I became depressed and lonely and as if my life was really taking a turn for the worse. I was about an hour and a half away from Tulsa, the life I knew, the friends I knew and missed, and the ability to go where I wanted when I wanted.

I stopped taking my insulin, not because I consciously

wanted to get sick, but because I was at a place in my life where I was so severely unhappy that I just didn't care anymore. I am a juvenile diabetic which means I don't produce insulin on my own, not even a little bit. My pancreas doesn't work. I've been diabetic since age 4. I went several days without taking a shot, probably 5 or 6 days. When I started feeling really sick, I was thirsty all the time, couldn't drink enough all day. I wasn't eating anything because I felt so nauseas all the time, I could hardly get up to make it to work I was so tired and weak. One day I got off work and was supposed to meet my cousin, Shelle, at home. Instead I got in my car and drove myself to the emergency room in town. They tested my blood and it was normal, when I say normal, it was about 100. They couldn't find anything wrong and I did not tell them I hadn't had insulin in days. I figured if my blood sugar was normal then I must just be sick.

That evening I went back to ER because I began throwing up everything I drank. And I was drinking everything within reach all the time. I didn't tell anyone; I just went by myself. Worrying my Gran-gran seemed like the wrong thing to do. The hospital did another blood test & then sent me home with a prescription for nausea medicine. I went home that night and started noticing that it was difficult for me to concentrate or think or really feel like I was in control of myself at all, but I finally slept. The next day I slept all day until mid-afternoon when I got dressed and went to work. I worked until about 8 that evening and felt so lethargic after that I again went to ER. Same thing, different day. I felt myself dying inside but they could find nothing wrong, and I wondered why my blood sugar still read normal to them. As I left the hospital this evening, I stopped at a local 7-11 to get a drink because I was still very thirsty, which is a sign of high blood sugar. I remember parking but I remember nothing else. What happened next, I can only tell you from what witnesses say. Two men were in the 7-11 who knew my cousin, and so knew me as well. They saw me passed out in my car and came over to see if I needed help. From what I'm told, they couldn't get me to talk, but they knew where I lived so one boy drove my car to get me home and the other followed him in their car.

I vaguely remember getting to the house and my cousin, Shelle, coming out and being a bit rude and I could tell she was mad or angry with me. I was so out of sorts that I didn't ask her or care. They made sure I got inside, explained what had happened and left. I still don't know who those boys were, but I am thankful they got me home. I remember laying on the sofa in the big living room and asking to please call my Mom, who I hadn't talked to since I began getting sick. Someone gave me the phone and I told Mom something about being really sick and I thought I was dying, I loved her & I'd talk to her tomorrow. After that, I hung up and my world went black. My gran-gran says I peed myself and they couldn't wake me up, so they called my Mom & she told them to call an ambulance. I can't even explain the feeling, I guess it was just like being in a fog and not being able to see clearly or think clearly.

Remember I am completely passed out, so I recollect none of this, but this is what my family has told me. At the hospital they took a urine test to check for ketones in my urine. My blood came back with sugar levels over 1200. Normal is somewhere between 80-120 so this is far greater than it should be. I was in a coma. I remember bits and pieces of being in a coma so I will share them with you now.

Everything was dark, there was no light, but I heard certain voices and I don't know if it was hours into this or days into it, I remember hearing my Mom's voice most, talking to me like I was there. I remember her talking to my Uncle Tom too. I remember my sister Shauna, who was 9, feeding me something, I hear it was jello. I remember Mom saying it was time for her to leave and I wanted so badly to tell her not to go and that I loved her, but I couldn't see or speak no matter how hard I tried. I felt myself cry inside but no tears came out. I was in a coma 4 or 5 days I guess from what I'm told, then one day my eyes opened. I'm really unclear on thing after that too. I remember a nurse coming in and seeing family come in and sleeping a lot.

To tell about this is hard because there are so many hours that I can't explain. I never saw what everyone says is "the light". I saw blackness, but a peaceful blackness. I knew there was a light far above me and I knew that in that light were my mom and my sisters and all the other people who loved me and whom I loved.

I heard them. I remember my mother telling me she loved me, and she had to go. I felt the tears and the longing. The ache that burned in my stomach and my throat. I tried so hard to speak. It was as though a zipper had been closed across my mouth. My hands couldn't move, and my mouth couldn't speak but I knew the words I wanted to say. I couldn't get them out and I was angry. I wanted her to know that I loved her, and I didn't want her to leave without knowing.

What if I never found my way out of this hole I was in? No matter how much I wanted to go into that very small light I saw way up there, I couldn't get there. I couldn't move. Then somehow, four days later, I was almost pushed into it. Something pushing me so hard into that hole. And I remember breathing and it hurt so much to take that breath, but I took it. And I was home again.

And somehow, I was ok. I took a couple months to feel better again but I made this miraculous full recovery. No brain damage and no repercussions for what had happened to me. And I found a new reason to live. I had hurt my family twice now. Scared them beyond anything understandable. So much pain in two years' time and still they stood strong.

After I came out of the coma, I moved back to Tulsa and stayed with April and Ray downtown at Ray's house. I got a job working as a manager at the Subway downtown for a friend. I enjoyed it, it was busy, and the customers were always nice, and the hours were amazing. I was always off by 5 or 6 in the evening.

The next couple of months I was really feeling good, I felt healthy and happy and as though things felt right for once. I wasn't eating well and hadn't been since I came out of the coma.

Even a food commercial on TV made me feel sick. I lost a lot of weight over the next few months. Other than my issue with eating though, I was feeling on top of the world.

April and I moved to a duplex in Tulsa in November of 1997. It was old and had an old bathtub with legs and a floor furnace, so it was always cold in the bedroom. But the house was good enough for us. Christmas came and went and then it was New Years. I think April stayed with Ray that night and I went to stay the night with Mom in Owasso.

I don't remember a lot about that night but at some point, I went home on New Year's Day. The house smelled funny and the neighbor or landlord told me something had happened while April and I weren't home. They said that our duplex had caught fire, the neighbors had smelled the smoke and called the fire department. They had to break open our front door to get in since no one was home. The fire had started from the floor furnace between the kitchen and living room. We had complained to the landlord about the furnace never shutting off and how it would get burning hot sometimes.

It had burned the side of the couch and a few things on the fireplace mantel, but it wasn't too bad, at least no one was home, no one was hurt, and not much was burned. The floor where the furnace was looked like a big hole now and the floor was burned all around it. Everything in there smelled horrible, I mean everything. Our clothes smelled awful even though we washed all of them, we had to throw a lot away.

We stayed there until March 1998 and then we moved out together. April needed a change, time away from Ray, and I was just along for the ride. I had nothing holding me down, no boyfriend, kids, pets, etc. I went everywhere April went really. My sister was my best friend. We planned on moving out in April 1998, but we didn't know where.

Moving to Vegas

In March of 1998 we took a trip with a girl friend of ours to Las Vegas. It was the best week we'd had in a long time, after my coma and April's breakup and the fire. When we got home, April decided she wanted to move to Las Vegas and after some coaxing she talked me into coming with her. She went to Vegas and rented an apartment and got us jobs lined up and then came home and we both finished packing. Howard, Mom's husband, and his friend, Mike agreed to drive us to Vegas with the U-Haul trailer and our two cars and help us get settled into our new life. Saying goodbye to my Mom was the hardest thing I ever had to do. My Mom was always close to me, I saw her often, and now I was moving 1200 miles away. This was our new life for now. I planned on being in Vegas a year or so and moving home.

I got a job at Motown Cafe inside New York, New York hotel & casino as a hostess and I liked it. I worked there for the summer and then worked in the office at All Star Café, where April worked. Vegas was beautiful and sunny and had palm trees. Oklahoma didn't have palm trees, they were pretty. Jobs were easy to find in Vegas back then. When All Star Café closed its doors in early 1999, I got a job working at a new hotel & casino being built called Venetian.

The first several months we worked out of a small office until the casino was built. Then in March of 1999 I had a car wreck, it was raining as I got on the highway and my tires slid from the oil-based asphalt they used in Vegas because of the heat. I slid sideways and blacked out. When I woke up, I was in the grass in the center median between the two directions of traffic and I sighed in relief that I had made it without getting hit. Then as I breathed in it hurt really bad and I could not catch my breath and I felt dizzy. I touched my left ear and my hand was filled with blood.

Someone was yelling, "Are you okay?" and then call an ambulance. I felt cold air & noticed I was in the passenger seat of my car and the steering wheel was bent. Next thing I remember the paramedics were trying to pull me out of the car & cutting my clothes off of me and I blacked out again. I woke up in the hospital in a daze. I felt stiff and a deep ache, but I felt happy. My sister had come up and I remember talking to her about a pink boa for a Barbie & about Weebles, you know the round headed little wooden people. I was full of morphine & saying things that made no sense. As I woke up the nurse came in and said "you won't be able to walk for a while" but I only heard the part where she'd said I wouldn't be able to walk. I was scared and confused.

It turned out I had broken my tailbone, 3 ribs on my left side, fractured my pelvis in 12 places and broken a hip. I called my work (the Venetian) to let them know I would be out of work for about 3 months while I healed and went to rehab to walk again. The day after I got out of the emergency room and into a regular room at the hospital my boss brought me flowers and proceeded to tell me I was fired. So here I was in the hospital, unable to walk, and now with no job. My sister took me home about a week later after I had learned to use a walker to get up the stairs to my apartment. I didn't leave the apartment again for 3 months other than to see doctors or go to rehab. April paid rent & bills while I was unemployed and rehabilitating.

That's how it is in Las Vegas, if you can't work your job goes to someone else. She did tell me that if they had anything available when I got better than they would hire me back. But really that isn't a promise and I couldn't set my hopes on that happening.

It took me three months to recover from my wreck and I still wasn't completely healed, I still hurt and walking long distances made me sore and tired. But in August I called my old boss at the Venetian and asked if there were any jobs available in the department I had worked in before.

She said yes that I could come back to my old position, which was basically doing payroll for the table games dealers, adjusting hours, and making sure they got paid. I was happy to go back to work and start making money again. April had been supporting me for the last three months and I felt bad.

I loved my job, but there was terrible tension between me and Mary, my boss. It was almost like she was mad at me for getting my job back after being gone so long. She was constantly calling me into her office about something I did wrong or angry that I had to take longer to run her errands because I still walked slow.

I ended up having a big blowout with her. I only put up with so much bullshit at any job before I will simply find something else. I had skills and a great personality, and I was smart. I could easily find another job. What I couldn't handle was being upset or stressed out or worried at work. Wondering if she was going to yell at me every day, having so much anxiety about my job that it made me nauseas and affected my quality of life.

So, I ended up losing my job. I got fired, because I stood up to my boss and told her I was not her slave and she needed to learn how to treat people. I should have been fired. I'm not making excuses. But after I lost that job I finished recovering and found a job that was closer to our apartment because I had no car anymore.

Las Vegas does have an excellent transportation system and it ran all day and all night. I was still able to go everywhere I wanted to go without having to ask anyone. I rode a lot of buses. I found a job I could walk to and stayed there until early 2000.

Mom was pregnant in 1999 and in early 2000 I decided to move home and help her with my new baby sister, Tori. I was there maybe 2 months when April asked me to come back out. She had gotten married and her husband was traveling so she needed company.

I was working at the Wal-Mart in Owasso, so I had nothing

great going on and Mom seemed to be doing fine, so I decided to go back to Vegas and be with April. I moved back and to be honest I had missed Vegas and April, so I was happy to be back. I transferred to the Wal-Mart in Vegas and moved up quickly within the company.

I had lots of friends there since it's a big store and there are tons of people working there. I became head of Customer Service and primarily worked over there doing refunds and returns. I enjoyed that. Then I applied for a CSM position which was a manager position though a low manager, it still meant more responsibility and a raise.

I met a manager there named Brian and we dated for a couple of months, but it didn't feel serious and I just enjoyed hanging out with him, but there wasn't really a connection.

Then I met a guy, Eddie, and he wanted to go out, but I knew he was young because he had just graduated high school and I think I was about 25. So, I just kind of blew him off over and over again. And then one day he sent me this card and had written a poem in it that made me laugh. It was so cute, and I knew he had written it himself.

By 2001 April and her husband, Aaron, had moved to St. Louis or somewhere like that. His job had him traveling and moving a lot. I was living in a 2-bedroom apartment with a friend we called, Corky. We had known each other since I had moved to Vegas and April had married his best friend. I had decided to stay in Las Vegas and Corky had too. We both worked a lot but got along like family.

Eddie and I began as friends, we would hang out with some other people we knew from Wal-Mart. He was quiet and sweet and smiled a lot. He sent me flowers almost every day when we first started dating. He was really nice, and he paid lots of attention and did everything for me. He didn't have a car, but I remember he would ride his bike everywhere. He lived with his grandparents and would ride all the way to my apartment to see me before work.

Eddie said he was twenty when we met, but I went to pick

him up one night and his grandpa was yelling at him and banging on the hood of my car. Eddie said he was just in a bad mood, but it freaked me out. Then Eddie told me he was enlisting into the Marines so he could not come by during the day anymore.

I was fine with that but started thinking it was weird that he had to go meet with his recruiter every morning. I had never known anyone who had to do that before. So, I talked to one of his friends about it and he laughed and said Eddie was taking summer school to get his diploma.

So, I asked Eddie to show me his driver license and he showed it to me, and Eddie was 18. Almost 19 because his birthday was in June and this was around May. I was mad at first, why was he lying to me? Suddenly it made sense why his grandpa would get so mad at me when I picked Eddie up so late at night or brought him home late. It was because he was still a kid and they were trying to get him to graduate.

Eddie and I had been together for several months though and I forgave him for lying to me. He was legal so I wasn't breaking any laws. That was the main reason I had been upset in the first place. That and why he would lie about something like that, since I would obviously find out he wasn't in the Marines.

Eddie and I were really good at the beginning. Then things changed and they changed really fast. Corky was going to move to St. Louis to live with April and Aaron, so I was looking for roommates to get an apartment with. Eddie said he would be my roommate and our friend, Ian, from work said he would too.

So, when Corky moved and our lease was up, I moved to a three-bedroom apartment with Eddie and Ian. I really had great thoughts about how it was going to be living with Eddie and Ian. But things rarely go the way you think they will, and this was no exception.

We all worked at Wal-Mart and everything was perfect in the beginning. We would all go to work together, and it was fun. Then we always were together if we went out and if we stayed in, there was always company and you couldn't be lonely.

But of course, it didn't last. First, Ian had always lived with his grandparents and wasn't used to having to pay rent or bills. He always got paid and would disappear all night, because he would go to the casino and gamble his entire paycheck away. I was constantly paying more than my share of everything. This wasn't as big of a problem as the fact that he was schizophrenic and had to take numerous medications every day or else he would do weird things, hear voices, and get really sick.

He had locked himself in his room for a couple days and hadn't shown up to work and finally Eddie and I went into his bedroom and found him curled up on his bed like a baby. We asked him what was going on and he tried to explain that he was hearing voices again. It's hard to understand the disease if you don't see it every day, but it turned out he had stopped taking his medication, so we called his grandparents not really knowing what to do.

They came and picked him up and we didn't hear from anyone for almost a week. They had taken him to the hospital and his doctor put him back on his medicine and I guess it took a few days, but he was better. His grandparents brought him home to their house to watch him for a couple of days and then brought him back to our apartment. They told us it is quite common for schizophrenics to stop taking their medicine because they think they don't need it. They think everyone else is lying to them and that the voices they hear are real.

They said just to make sure he was taking his medicine every day and to call if it happened again. It was scary. We were all young and didn't really know about psychological illnesses. But he seemed like the Ian that we knew and loved so we just left it at that.

And Eddie, he was great in the beginning but then started hanging out with some bad kids at work. You know the ones who stole, slept around, and partied a lot. Eddie started staying out all night, sometimes he didn't even come home. He called a number of times to have Ian or I come get him and wouldn't even know whose house he was at.

At some point during the two years we lived in that apartment, I flew home to see my family in Oklahoma. Before I left, days before I left, I found out that Eddie had been talking to s girl named Debbie who was his Mom's age, he was only 19 or 20. She had sent him numerous letters and taken some nude photos and some clothed photos that were just inappropriate.

She had even sent him numerous pairs of panties sprayed heavily with her perfume. He had also been telling her he was a professional skydiver, which he obviously wasn't. I read a lot of their letters and emails to each other and he told her a lot of lies. But in one of his latest emails he had talked to her about flying to Vegas to see him. She lived in Pennsylvania.

He told her I was a roommate so yet another lie. He was planning to fly her in to visit him at the exact same time I would be in Oklahoma. But I wasn't going to cancel my trip for this, so I still left as planned. I think I ended up telling Mom about all this stuff I had found out about Eddie. I had taken pictures of the letters and emails and panties, etc. Mom and I talked and after being there a week, I decided I would fly home early and see if this girl had actually flown in to see him.

So, I flew home and got home, and he wasn't home. I didn't know where he was, but I unpacked and talked to Ian. He said he had been at his grandparents, so he didn't know where Eddie was. Eddie came home the next day, shocked that I was home, but he was alone.

Not being one to shy away from problems, I confronted him. He tried to deny it until I showed him that I had found all the letters and the panties and emails. Back then on computers you could pull up history and it would show who someone had talked to, pages they visited, photos they looked at, etc. I had saved all of the ones I had found.

So, I know you are thinking I must be crazy to play detective like that. It was just an instinct. Things were turning strange with Eddie and he was on my computer a lot, I mean all night long. I would get up for work and he would still be up from the night before. He still acted like it was no big deal and said he wouldn't talk to her anymore.

But he had been talking to this woman for two years, longer than we had been dating. I contacted her on myspace I think it was, but it could be a different site. She said they had been talking for a long time, he said he had dated me, but we were just roommates now, he had lied to her about his age and his job. He had lied to me about his age when I met him. For the first year we dated he said he was 20, but he was only 18. I won't even begin to tell you how I found out the truth about his age.

Eddie was a compulsive liar; he really couldn't stop himself. He lied about anything and everything. It could be something small and stupid, but he'd lie about it. This Debbie didn't care who I was, she said that was between Eddie and I, but she was going to keep talking to him and sending him things. Eddie had a P.O. Box so her letters wouldn't come to the apartment.   I didn't leave him, though looking back that was a dumb decision. I have to assume it was because I was young and thought he would change. That was only the first time I found out about his cheating. If you could call it cheating, it was more like a lack of respect for me.

We fought all the time after that and one night I remember throwing a 2-liter bottle of Pepsi at him and it blew up all over the wall. I had to clean it, so I didn't do that again, plus I missed his head. He went out that night with 3 girls from work who were very well known with the boys at work for obvious reasons. He didn't come home until the next afternoon.

When he came home, I told him I was leaving. I had enough of the bullshit and just didn't trust him at all anymore and I was sick of thinking people were calling me a fool for staying. I was a manager at work, and everyone knew Eddie had been hanging out with these girls and partying all night.

He was yelling at me and was calling one of the girls during our argument and telling her she could move in because I was moving out. I was pissed off. I ran into his room and grabbed the phone out of his hand and hung up on her. He got angry and pushed me really hard and I grabbed his beaded curtain to keep from falling and I fell anyway and took the curtain with me.

Then I got up and was crying and before I had time to do anything, he ran at me and pushed me really hard, knocking me through the wall in the hallway. My body left a huge whole in the wall and I fell to the floor. I couldn't catch my breath he had pushed me so hard into the wall that my chest was on fire and my back was shooting pain and I thought I was going to suffocate because I just couldn't breathe.

Ian was in the living room and had seen me get pushed through the wall and got up and came running asking what the hell was going on. I was still on the floor in the middle of the hallway and just said I need to go to the hospital. I was in horrible pain and thought he hurt me really bad.

Ian and Eddie both drove me to the hospital and said to call when I was done, and they left. I didn't really think about it at the time but I'm sure he didn't go in with me because he knew he would be in trouble. I walked in and was seen right away. I had torn some muscle in my back and had bruised ribs which is why it hurt to breathe.

They asked me what happened and before thinking I told them my boyfriend had pushed me through a wall. A few minutes later the police were there asking me if I wanted to press charges and taking a statement. I said that no, I did not want to press charges. So, I finished filling out my statement and then called Ian to pick me up and told him not to bring Eddie because the police were still there.

I was in terrible pain for a few weeks and could barely walk. But I kept working and everyone there knew what had happened and were mad at Eddie. Then a few days later an officer & detective showed up at my apartment. They asked if Eddie was there and I said no. I felt this sick feeling in my stomach wondering why they wanted Eddie if I wasn't pressing charges.

Then they asked to come in, so I let them in, I was home alone. They said they needed to take pictures of my wall and needed a statement from Eddie to close the report. I took the detective's card and they left. When Eddie came home from work and I told him, he freaked out and screamed at me.

I told him they just had to get his side of the story so they could close the report, and that they knew I was not pressing charges. He was scared, I remember because they knocked on the door a couple different times and he wouldn't let me answer it. His Mom called me because he had called her to see what she thought he should do. I told her I did not plan on pressing charges and that he just needed to call this detective so he would stop knocking on our door.

She got mad at me and said Eddie didn't push me, that her son would never do that. I told her we had been fighting and told her the story and that yes, he had pushed me through a wall in the hallway. She basically called me a liar, which made me mad, but she was in Ohio and I was here and knew what happened.

The only thing she said that I should have listened to was when she said that Eddie and I just weren't right for each other and shouldn't be together. But young and dumb won that argument. I hung up the phone and when Eddie came home from "hiding out" with friends, I told him to call this guy. So finally, he called him back and gave him a statement and that was that.

He said we were done since I didn't want to press charges, but the State could pursue it if they looked at the evidence and felt they needed to. My memory fails me, but I think we actually met with him in person.

Needless to say, once our lease ended, we moved into another apartment together. Eddie never hit me again, I think that scared him a lot. He always brought it up and blamed me saying I had done this to him. I felt really bad but all I had wanted was to be treated.

Things were okay in the new place. I don't have many memories of it. I've just lost a lot of my memory since the stroke so some things I remember clearly and other things I can't recall at all.

April was now living in Grapevine, TX with Aaron, Corky and their new baby Kendall. I missed having her around. April and I had done everything together since the day we were born. She was my best friend and she was smart about men. I wasn't at all, so I called her a lot for advice.

Eddie and I started fighting again in 2003 and I finally decided I was going to move to Texas and stay with April. I think it was actually Eddie who said I needed to move to Texas. He said he needed time away from me and I should leave. So, April paid for a U-Haul and some of the construction guys loaded all my stuff into it in a few hours.

I was working at American West Homes by then and they were truly kind to me. They were willing to help me get an apartment without Eddie if I wanted to stay. Something bad had happened with Eddie but I can't really remember what. I think the state had him picked up for a bench warrant on the domestic violence thing that had happened. So, he spent the night in jail and his Mom bailed him out and hated me.

She demanded I move out and she was going to move in when I left. Yes, I remember now. Eddie's Mom and sister hated me then. I think only because they thought I got him put in jail, when it was the State who did it, not me.

But I was pretty much forced out and having no family in Vegas at that time and him having his Mom, sister and soon his brother just moving to Vegas, I was no match. I didn't see the point in trying to defend myself against someone who clearly thought I was lying about her son.

So, April paid for the truck and we put my car on a trailer behind this huge truck. And I drove from Las Vegas to Grapevine, TX all by myself. It was terrible, I was emotional, I hoped I wouldn't get lost, my phone had no service most of the time, and the truck broke down three times making my trip take three days and having to stay in two hotels. And in Wichita Falls, TX I had to stop for my third breakdown, and I stopped at a rest stop, so people were around, and I waited. This semi-truck driver came around and said he was going to sit with me and had called the police because there was a man hiding behind the picnic benches, half naked, jerking off and looking at me.

I freaked out; I hadn't even seen this man. The truck driver said he had been pulling out when he noticed him and then saw me sitting there by myself. The police showed up in a few minutes and talked to the truck driver and arrested the other guy. He had escaped from some mental hospital in Wichita Falls. Seriously, I couldn't make this stuff up, it really happened.

Marriage

I arrived in Grapevine on June 3, 2003. I remember because it was Aaron's birthday and I met them at the apartment and immediately went out for dinner and drinks. I was relieved to finally be there.

My heart was empty though, having to leave Vegas the way I did. Not really wanting to start things over in a new town but being pretty much pushed out of my old one. But I absolutely loved being with April again and I got to finally spend lots of time with my niece, Kendall. She was about 18 months old and the cutest little baby ever.

I spent all my time with her when I wasn't at work. We ate together and played together, and I sang her to sleep every night. This is why Landslide by Stevie Nicks is our song, because when I sang it to her, she'd get quiet and stare at me and smile.

I can't even put my love for this baby girl into words. She changed my whole life. She loved me so much and it made me feel so special. Kendall was my shining star. She took all my pain away and made me so happy just hearing her laugh.

I was in Texas for almost five months, had made some great friends and was doing good on my own. Then I decided to go home to Vegas for my birthday and visit with my friends. I met Eddie at the airport, and he was standing there in a white suit and flowers.

All the feelings that I had finally gotten rid of were back. I ran to him and hugged him. That night I stayed in my hotel and he came by for a while and watched TV. The next day, I met up with some girlfriends. We all went out that evening and hung out at the apartment till early in the morning.

The next day was my birthday. Eddie and I went to the mall

then I went to get my hair done with Wendy. It was a fun day. Then Eddie and I decided to get married ... it was Vegas, I loved him again and we were having so much fun the past two days.

That day was my 28th birthday on October 30, 2003. Wendy and her husband James said they would be witnesses and Eddie told his Mom. She seemed happy about it, which was weird to me, but I didn't care at that moment. I was getting married.

We went to a chapel near the courthouse and were married by a little Asian man. Eddie's Mom paid for wedding pictures, so we took pictures and then went to the courthouse to get our marriage license. Then we went to TGI Friday's and drank and ate with about ten of our friends.

The next morning, I felt sick inside, like what have I done. And didn't know how I was going to tell my family. But I called April and told her that Eddie and I were going to fly to Texas together and pack my thing and drive back to Vegas. We flew together back to Texas to pack my things, kiss my beautiful niece, Kendall, goodbye, and drive back to Vegas. I cried most of the trip. I didn't know if I had made the right choices and I was painfully heart-broken at leaving my baby niece. We didn't even have rings, I had to buy our rings from a shop in Texas and have them mailed to me. Eddie only wore his for a week before he said he had lost it. I should have taken it as a sign that this was far from a good marriage. But if there was one thing I was, it was stubborn. My marriage would not fail, I would not be a statistic.

Eddie left the first time after 5 months of marriage. When we got married, I had a 2 bedroom apartment & he moved his friend in with us. I wasn't happy about it and he would have girls over & music blasting in his room all night. He did drugs too. Eddie started doing them with him, spending more & more time going out & coming home at 7am when I was leaving for work. Marriage was a mess. As much as I loved him, I kicked him out or he left, one of the two, and I ended up with a couple months left on a 2-bedroom apartment.

He ended up having to leave the apartment. I remember now. He had been at work at House of Blues and I suspected he was cheating so I had driven up to his work and stayed in the parking garage until he got off work. I just wanted to see if he left work and came home or if he met someone and came home later after cheating on me.

My phone rang and it was him, about the same time I saw him walk to his car and start driving away. He said he was working late and would be home in a couple of hours. Hmmmmm, really? I didn't tell him, but I was following him. He had already told lie number one.

He pulled up to a house in a small neighborhood. I just watched as he got out and went inside. I didn't see who answered the door. I called him and asked him where he was, and he said he was still at work. So, I asked him if he was at work then why was he at whatever address this was? He got really mad and asked me how I knew where he was and was like "Are you spying on me?".

Then he came outside and told me on the phone that I was going to regret doing that. He got in his car, didn't even come over to my car, and sped away in a hurry. I was crying and driving home. He had hung up on me. Then he called back and told me I better not come home, and I told him that was my home too and that he couldn't make me leave.

He said I better not come home, or I was going to regret it. What was I going to regret? It was my apartment, all my clothes were inside, I had to work in the morning, I was going home. I told him he could leave if he wanted but that I was on my way home so if he didn't want to see me, he better goes stay with a friend.

Eddie was calling me every name imaginable and he was angry. Was it because I caught him lying … again? He said if I came home, he was calling the police. I guess for harassment. He hung up on me. So, I called the police station and asked if an officer could meet me at the apartment because I wasn't sure what Eddie was going to make me regret or even if he was going to let me in. He was acting erratic and blaming me anyway. Saying it was me being a psycho.

So, the dispatcher told me to wait for an officer at the apartment office and not to go to the apartment until he got there. He was there in about ten minutes and then we drove to my apartment. Eddie was inside because his car was there. So, we went to the apartment and I opened the door.

Eddie and his friend, Franco, were inside. He was quiet when he saw the officer and then said I needed to leave. The officer said I lived there and had rights to be there. Eddie started yelling at the officer. Then the cop said he could leave for the night so maybe things would settle down.

There is a lot to this incident and things had been building up ever since the day we got married. The officer asked him if he had said not to come home or I'd regret it, and he said no. At this point Eddie was yelling and just really being stupid and mad. The cop asked me if he could see the texts and listen to the voicemails and I let him. He had separated us and had Eddie with another officer. He listened to all the voicemails I had and had both of us write statements. He then said I could go back in the apartment.

By this time, our friends who also lived in the apartments had come outside and Wendy came over by me and James was trying to calm Eddie down. I went inside with Wendy and a few minutes later the officer knocked on the door and said they were arresting Eddie. I asked him why, I really didn't want him going to jail, I just wanted to go to bed and for him to stop being stupid.

The officer said they had a warrant for him. So, they took him, and I cried. I knew he was going to blame me for this, and I thought he would probably leave me. He had somehow managed to make me feel like it was my fault, that I was psycho. Not just this night but every time we got in a fight or every time I caught him cheating.

Turned out he had a bench warrant for that domestic thing that had happened a while back. The State had tried to press charges I guess, and he never showed up for court. That really didn't surprise me, but I knew he was going to be really mad at me for it, even though I had never ever pressed charges or pursued anything.

Eddie's Mom bailed him out the next morning. He was mad and said none of this would have happened if he'd never met me. I felt horribly guilty and sad. I really thought it was my fault and didn't blame him for leaving. Thinking back, I should have divorced his ass then. Because before it was all said and done there would be all kinds of lies, women, bad friends, and drugs.

He moved out after his Mom bailed him out of jail. He stayed with her, but I think it took them months to pick up his things. I had to put it in storage and pay for that for several months because even though I had asked them to come get his things, they never did.

April and Aaron and Corky and little Kendall were planning to move back to Vegas. I was an emotional wreck over Eddie and so April's husband drove down from Grapevine, TX and stayed with me while he found a house. My apartment was pretty empty since I had moved Eddie's stuff and packed most of mine. We only had about a month left on the lease, so I was still staying there for now. Aaron found a house to rent really fast and flew back to Texas to start packing. Soon we all moved in together, April, Aaron, Corky, Kendall and me. The next few years are a blur, but Kendall became like my own child. She was my best friend in the world, there was no one who would take her place.

Eddie, through the years, would come in and out of my life. I wouldn't have a clue when he was leaving to pursue some other girl or decide to spend every night with his friends out looking for trouble. I loved him so much and blamed myself constantly for why he would rather be with his friends all night or why he took up drug use or why he needed to cheat all the time. I didn't know why he hid from his work that he was married or why he did what he did. It always made me feel inferior, just not good enough to be a wife. If he was not ashamed of me, I sure took it that way. Maybe I should have been younger or more beautiful or thinner, maybe I just wasn't really good enough for anyone.

My thinking had progressively gotten worse about myself. I worked and spent time on the computer, grocery shopped and did the laundry and tried to keep house and just waited for him to come back home.

I always gave all I could to my marriage, which is really hard to do when you have a ghost for a husband. Sure, I had his last name, but I had nothing else. We had no pictures of us together other than a few wedding pictures. We didn't have a home together, none of his clothes were in the closet, no toothbrush in the bathroom. It was a marriage only to me, not to friends and certainly not to him.

I can't explain the heartbreak or loss I felt. The sheer loneliness, trying to be faithful and a good wife with nothing to show for it. I didn't date, didn't go out, I spent every day with my Kendall and waited. What I was waiting for, I don't know. I expected married life to be so different. I thought it would be me and him against all odds, we'd be together, have a home, maybe kids, though having kids came and went quickly in my mind, knowing he'd never be a good father to kids.

It was sad really, why I allowed him to make me feel like I was so wrong for crying when he didn't come home, or when he lied to me about where he was going after work, or told me I was crazy for contacting girls and letting them know he was married. It was my fault he did everything he did. And I know it sounds crazy, but it affected me, the man I loved and married telling me how I was crazy and that's why he did these things. I believed I was really doing something wrong. Then I was informed by a person I didn't know, who called my cell phone to talk to me about Eddie, that some really horrible things were going on that I could never have imagined. I can't even say what those things were because I don't want to ruin anything for him in his own life. But it changed everything for me, left me feeling completely numb and wondering who my husband really was.

My final straw, besides the call from this person, was that he stopped calling completely for several weeks. I found out after a couple months that he had left his clothes and everything at his Mom's place and gone to San Francisco to be with some girl he had met on one of his visits there.

She had just had a baby and met Eddie and I guess he had been cheating with her too. She talked him into moving in with her at some point and just left yet again. It didn't last long, I guess she decided to go back to her baby's daddy and kicked Eddie out on the streets of San Francisco. He called me and said he was coming back to Vegas.

I talked to him for a couple weeks while he moved back, and I think moved in with his Mom again. But the love I had for him didn't feel the same. I just couldn't spend any more of my time worrying, being emotionally broken, giving chances, ruining my own life, and giving all my love to someone who said he loved me but showed it in really hurtful ways.

I loved him deeply, and it took five years and him running off to San Francisco & Seattle for me to finally say it was over and ask for a divorce. I was torn apart inside but tried so hard to hide it. I printed all the paperwork from online and filled everything out and checked it and double checked it and triple checked it. Then I told him I wanted a divorce and to meet me at the notary and sign the paperwork, and he did. After he signed it, having absolutely no emotion, but why would he? He had been living like a single man our entire marriage, this was nothing that would change his life. So, after he signed, I made all the copies and kept one, gave him one and took the other to the courthouse.

Walking into the courthouse alone, with a line of men waiting to file their own paperwork, I waited for my turn. I had done everything right, checked & rechecked that everything was proper, and filed my divorce papers. A week later, on September 17th, 2008 I got my divorce papers back in the mail, signed by the judge ... I was officially divorced. I mailed Eddie a copy of the signed paperwork and kept the other.

On my own now. What was the worst that could happen,

my marriage was never two people living together in a house making plans for a family. He never supported me or paid my bills. As devastated as I was, I was no worse off! But it wasn't long after the divorce was final when Eddie started coming over often and staying the night, playing with little Kendall who loved her Uncle Eddie.

I was torn between letting him back in my life and dating this friend of mine from where I worked at an Insulation company. He was such a great guy, this man I was dating. He really was so completely different from Eddie. He took me out to dinners, weekend trips, parties, he loved Kendall and loved taking her with us places. He had a daughter about her age. He bought me things and complimented me all the time. He put a new radio in my car. He brought me soup when I was sick. I really can't say enough good things about him.

But even with everything I had with him there were things that both of us still had to deal with. He was going through a divorce, still living with his wife in separate rooms and trying to raise their little girl and keep everything civil. I was trying to move on from a terrible marriage yet fighting my feelings of love and what I knew as familiar with Eddie. It was so complicated, and the man I was dating was very much wanting to be married again and have more kids and be more serious. In the end I broke up, mainly because he needed to get a divorce and work through some emotional changes that divorce comes with. I thought he was great, but the timing was terrible. I didn't want another marriage or a family. I had just had a horrifying marriage and was jaded by love and commitment and needed to be alone.

Years of reflection have changed the pain of marriage & my resentment of Eddie into a vast source of learning and growing and being able to forgive him in every way.

So, I chose to move home to Oklahoma in April of 2009, away from Vegas and all the painful memories. But with that came the most crushing pain ever in my life, leaving Kendall, who was now 7. I had to go because I had to be far away from Eddie so he couldn't somehow slip back into my life.

Kendall and I cried a lot that last month before I left. This little girl was my everything, my best friend, my partner, my baby. She slept with me one last night & cried and asked me not to leave her. I cried and she cried until we both fell asleep. March 9th Mom & I began driving back to Oklahoma and I cried for the first several hours, not knowing what I was going back too. I was afraid and alone in those fears but knew to change my life I had to do it.

2009 in Oklahoma

So, April of 2009 Mom and I make it to Oklahoma after stay-ing the night outside of Texas. It felt good to be back. Quiet, no busy streets, sirens, lights, mobs of people. I missed my sister & Kendall, mostly at night I would talk to Kendall on the phone and go to bed in tears. Plus, I still missed Eddie and didn't know, at this point, how my life would go or if I'd be alone forever. I got a temporary job with Borden doing some accounting work, within two weeks of moving home, and held that job for about 3 months. I got an apartment close to Mom's house and got to visit with my Aunt and Grandparents a lot more. Family kept me from falling into depression and crying too much for my old life. This was my new beginning, my time to start again with people who didn't know my past, about my marriage or about my life before.

I began dating about a month after getting to Oklahoma, an old high school friend and someone I really liked. He under-stood that I had just gone through a divorce and he was in the middle of one himself. Life was moving forward, and I had re-connected with some of my high school friends.

I had a lot of pain still, mistrust, I didn't know how I felt about the concept of love. I felt a little out of my element all the time. I missed Eddie, well I think I missed companionship and understanding and feeling like I had someone to look out for me. April was gone and Kendall, my entire world was differ-ent and that's a hard pill to swallow.

Life felt better after several months, I was settling into Okla-homa and seeing old friends and meeting new ones. I had a job working for Trawick Construction as the office manager. It was a small office with just three of us and some foremen in the warehouse. But it was a full-time job with decent pay and nice people, so I enjoyed it.

My dating relationship with Jason was not really moving well. Understandably, his wife had just left him in April, and he was having a really tough time. And they had two children, so I know it was tearing him up. He wasn't really looking for a girl-friend and I knew he dated others, and I just wasn't sure what I needed, but I wanted to be with someone exclusive and sort of ready or willing to consider something more serious.

In August of the same year I went out with some high school friends, we were going to see Dave play in his band. He had been telling me to come to a show since I lived in Vegas and now that I was home, I thought I'd go.

It was so much fun and there were so many people that I knew there. It sounds funny saying this, but I immediately noticed the guy singing in Dave's band. I didn't know him, but a lot of my friends seemed to, I found out his name was Steve. He was cute, my first thought was he must be a little older than me because he had some gray hair and I didn't remember him from school but the older people with me knew him.

I don't like dating guys who identify themselves as musicians because typically, for me anyway, that means they have a more reckless spirit, no real sense of commitment and unintention-ally tend to hurt people who love them too much.

After they were done with the show a bunch of us went to the bar down the street, Arnie's, and drank, smoked, and just talked for a couple hours. Steve came over there with some girl he was on a date with. I caught myself looking at him a couple times but turned away before he noticed. My friend, Mike, was with me and I wasn't looking to break up a couple anyway. After a couple hours everybody was ready to leave. I said goodnight and got in my car to drive home, but really wasn't tired yet. So, I phoned Dave and he said to come over to Steve's where some of them were hanging out, he said he would have Rob meet me at the gas station so I could follow him there.

So, I'm thinking to myself that this is really working out in my favor because I kind of wanted to find out more about this Steve guy anyway. So, I met up with Rob and followed him to Steve's house where Dave and some other guys from the band were getting ready to watch the show on videotape.

It ended up being a fun night, watching the video, talking, and then watching an old movie. I really liked this guy, just the little I knew of him. He didn't really pay attention to me or anything, but he seemed to be laid back, easy going and friendly. Seemed pretty perfect. But it was time to go, Dave was leaving and said I could follow him out, so I'd know where I was going, so I said goodbye & left.

When I got home, I got on Facebook and friended Steve since he'd kind of know who I was. I posted something about going to Cheap Trick in a couple weeks & if anyone wanted to go to let me know. A couple days later, I noticed he has responded that he'd love to go but had to work that night so I mentioned meeting for a drink after, and he said he would. That was my in.

After the drinks in mid-August, I think we just kept seeing each other. I wasn't seeing Jason anymore because he had stopped calling and brought a really young 20-year-old to Dave's last show. I didn't tell him I wasn't seeing him anymore since he probably knew since he had gone out with someone else. No, I was pretty into Steve from the beginning and really hadn't thought to date anyone else.

Don't misunderstand, I had a serious connection with Jason. We had a big connection; I couldn't hide from that. He had gotten to know me on a very deep level, and it was more than physical between us. The physical attraction to him was strong too. He is probably one of the best-looking guys I ever dated, even now.

I wish things had worked out with him, but like most of the relationships I tend to have, the timing was terrible, and he still loved his ex-wife. That and he liked dating young girls, much younger than me, and I didn't want to compete with any ladies who were 15 years younger than me and had firm bodies and perfect skin and no baggage. I was only 33 but wasn't going to compete for his love, fight for love, I would do over and over again, but I won't compete.

Steve

I met Steve by accident. I had promised my friend, Dave, that when I moved back to Oklahoma, I'd come watch his band play, so that's what I did. And after some friends were going to Steve's house to hang out and I went. That was pretty much it. I asked him to have a drink after a Cheap Trick show later that month and we just never really stopped seeing each other after that.

When I moved home from Las Vegas, it was after a divorce from a marriage that was anything but conventional. I had really loved my husband, really wanted things to work out for us. But after five years of lies, cheating, drugs, and him disappearing over and over, I couldn't deal with that pain any longer. I was broken. Even after I moved home to start over it was hard to want to be around friends, go out, smile, and pretend it was all okay.

I really thought that life was over for me. I didn't even think of dating, much less loving someone else. Steve was an accident. Even after the first couple of dates I told myself it was just fun and that was it.

But the thing about Steve was that he was just so nice, and I liked the way he looked at life. He didn't seem to be aggressive or think negative about anything. We were out all the time. We took trips to Kansas City, Eureka Springs, NASCAR in Texas, NASCAR at Talladega, and just had a really good time together.

Well, I fell for him hard and fast which I didn't want to do. He had moved into my apartment after only knowing him about eight months. This was fine with me, would help me out & him too since he was behind on his rent on his place by a few months. For me, it just meant more time with Steve without driving to Tulsa.

He spent Thanksgiving with my family and Christmas too. I really honestly thought our relationship was perfect. We never fought, we never argued, he was very laid back, a hard worker and I felt good about things. I went to all his shows just to support him. I just wanted to be sure he knew I was there for him and took an interest in what he did.

I was proud of him and proud to be with him. I admired him and liked his view on people and life and just everyday things. He was a huge flirt, I guess that would be the only thing I didn't care for. I don't think I ever brought it up, but he told me every time we were out that this girl was hot or that girl was hot. Girls on TV were hot and girls on the street were hot. He said he thought all girls had something hot about them. I handled it because if that was his only flaw then that was okay.

In October of 2010 we decided to move to an apartment in Tulsa to be closer to both our work. I think we moved in around the 28th. It was only days before my 35th birthday on October 30th. I remember being stressed out about Steve having to move everything alone because I had to work. But he said he could do it.

I came home from work really tired, I had a really awful headache and my chest felt tight, I didn't ever get headaches so I figured it was from being tired and the tightening in my chest was probably just acid reflux that I had suffered from for many years. When I walked in the door it would barely open. So I squeezed in. Steve had gotten everything moved in, it was all downstairs in the living room and dining room. Being tired and feeling like crap, I almost started crying.

Thinking back, I shouldn't have stressed out so bad, but I did, and I said something to Steve about it. I should have told him thank you for moving everything and moved on. I just felt sick and couldn't even find a sofa to sit down. He got mad and went upstairs to try to finish putting the bed together.

The next morning, I went to work. I can't remember if Steve had to work but he worked nights so even if he did he wouldn't leave until four. I felt less emotional about the move now and hoped Steve wasn't still mad at me. Moving in to a place in Tulsa, away from my Mom, and living and depending on Steve made me nervous. I didn't want to have anything go wrong, I had asked Steve a hundred times if he was sure he wanted to move in with me because if he wasn't I would just sign another lease in Owasso. After all, he hadn't had to pay rent for the time we lived at my apartment, he just helped with food and bills. Plus, he had been a bachelor for a long time and kind of a hermit before we met.

But he said we should do this, and I trusted him, so we did it. I went to work, and it was uneventful. I mean it was just a normal day. I still had this horrible headache and didn't really think about it, just thought maybe allergies, so I bought some Excedrin Migraine on my way home from work.

I moved things around and put things up after I got home and pretty much spent the next few days doing this. Saturday the 30th I believe it was, was Freaker's Ball and Steve's band would be playing along with lots of others. It was at Cain's Ballroom downtown and I had been before and knew it was fun. So, Steve had taken off work and I painted his face like a werewolf and then I dressed up as a witch. Everyone dressed up, it was a Halloween event.

I still had a pretty aggressive headache but took another pill and didn't think about it. I hadn't told Steve I was feeling sick because I didn't want to cause problems before his big show. This was also my birthday; I was turning 35 today. We didn't really celebrate it though. That was ok because I'd have fun going out tonight anyway and seeing friends.

We got to Cain's and met up with everyone. My good friend Matt came out to keep me company and have fun. I kept feeling dizzy and lightheaded during this event. I hadn't been drinking since I rarely drank at all. And I didn't want to miss Steve playing. So, they were on stage & Matt and I went over and listened. At some point I told Matt I needed to sit down for a minute, so we walked over to the bleacher seats I think, but we sat down somewhere. I felt nauseas and dizzy and my head was throbbing.

We sat for a little while; Matt went to the bathroom which took a while because of the long line. When he came out, I thought I could stand up and be okay, so we went and found the others. We hung out until really late, getting home around 4am. We were tired and I think we went straight to bed.

The next day was Halloween, and if my memory is correct, Steve's friend was getting married today and we had to dress up and go to their wedding. So, I helped Steve, who was going as a zombie and I was wearing my witch costume again. We went to the wedding and I really didn't know anyone because they were mostly kids who worked at Hideaway, but I had a good time and hung out with some of them while Steve socialized. It was late when we left and I don't really remember if we did anything after, but I think we just went home to bed because I worked on Monday morning.

I had been throwing up when I ate the past day or so, I figured it was just my Gastroparesis acting up. I still had that stupid headache too. I really hoped I would feel better soon, but I hadn't had much sleep over the weekend, so I probably needed sleep.

Tuesday was November 2nd, 2010 and I woke up to my alarm, Steve was asleep in bed, but had to work later. I got dressed and then went to the bathroom and brushed my teeth and hair. I always just put my makeup on in my car once I got to work. I don't know why; it was just what I did.

I was getting ready to walk downstairs at the apartment and suddenly felt sick and very dizzy. I took the first step and my legs seemed to just buckle under me and I ended up sliding all the way down to the bottom of the stairs. I sat there for a minute or so and then laughed at myself. I was glad no one saw me do that.

I put my shoes on and grabbed my phone and keys and went to work. I stopped and got my coffee before going in to work and then went in and opened all the doors, turned on the lights, the computers, machines and made coffee. I set up the conference room for the attorneys who had a meeting that day. Jamie came in and I talked to her a little. I loved Jamie, her husband was a retired cop and she was one of our attorney's assistants. She had been a paramedic before she hurt her back or her knee or something. My headache had gone away for the most part and I finally felt better. I told her how I had fallen down my stairs at home that morning and my left foot was hurting.

Later that day my foot and ankle were swollen, and it hurt more, but I worked the rest of the day and went home. Steve was at work. I settled in, got some food, and watched TV and fell asleep on the sofa until he got home. We stayed up till maybe 2am and went to bed.

I got up for work on Wednesday morning and felt a little sick still but went to work hoping it would go away. My ankle looked bad, mostly from swelling but I was clearly limping today and hadn't been the day before. I told Jamie it hurt more and if it didn't get better, I would see a doctor.

It was around mid-afternoon, and I was in our supply room making copies and the phone rand. I picked it up in there and tried to say our company's name and all these weird words came out of my mouth, I tried again, and it came out all wrong. Jamie walked by at about the same time and I remember giving her a blank look and said, "help me" and it sounded slurred. She came running and I got very dizzy and she walked me to a chair and made me drink a coke. A few minutes later I felt ok and couldn't figure out why that happened.

I finished working that day and went home, Steve was at work already, so I decided to do some laundry. I gathered up all the laundry and walked to the apartment laundry room which was down a bit and across from the office and downstairs in like a basement.

I put the laundry in and waited for it to wash before leaving. I figured I'd leave it in the dryers for a little while and walk home. So, I finally got it all in the dryer, there were like 3 loads since we had just moved and had extra laundry. I walked back to the apartment, and noticed these sharp, like electric shocks going up my left leg and my ankle hurt more. My limp was more like a drag of my left leg, it hurt so badly.

I watched a show and then went back to the laundry room, put all the clean clothes in my tall laundry hamper and went to leave, I was going to fold it at home. I tried to carry the hamper but for whatever reason I couldn't keep hold of it. So, I drug it with my right hand across the floor to the stairs.

My left hand felt weird, but I managed to grab the hamper with my left hand and the handrail with my right hand, but damn it was really hard to climb the stairs. It probably took me 20 minutes to get up the stairs. I started crying not knowing what was happening to me. I drug the hamper home because I couldn't carry it even though I had carried it there.

When I got into the apartment I was out of breath and exhausted, so I sat down, turned the TV to a show and didn't worry about the laundry. My leg was causing these electric, kind of irritating shivers through my body and I had to keep moving my body around trying to stop them. My foot had slight bruises, but didn't look broken, but maybe it was.

Steve got home around 11pm. I hadn't told him about what had happened at work really. He knew I had fallen down the stairs. I told him about the laundry and how I had a really hard time with it. My foot was throbbing, probably from walking on it so much. I felt terrible and couldn't get rid of these shivers that I kept having. He looked worried and finally I asked him to take me to the emergency room to look at my foot.

The hospital took my blood sugar first thing because I told them I was diabetic. It tested well at 128. So, they took me in for an x-ray to see if it was broken or anything. It took forever and I got impatient waiting in this room.

I couldn't lie down so I got up and walked around, or limped around, hoping these electric shivering things would stop because I just can't explain how horrible they felt. The doctor came in and said my foot was not broken and was probably just a strain. So, I said okay and told Steve I just wanted to go home. They left us in that room forever so when a nurse finally came in,

I told him I was going to leave if it wasn't broken.

Steve and I drove home and stayed up a few minutes and went to bed. Thursday morning, I went to work. But I felt horrible and Jamie saw me and said something was wrong. I couldn't walk without holding on to things and my speech sounded funny still. Some people couldn't tell but I knew my voice and I did not normally sound like this. She called paramedics and said it may be Bell's Palsy.

This little Asian guy was my doctor in the emergency room that day. I told him that my speech was slurred, and my leg was messed up. I told him we thought it was a stroke or Bell's Palsy. He said no I was too young for a stroke. He tested my blood sugar and I think it was about 200. It had been going up the last day or so because I felt sick. He said my speech sounded fine to him and I told him that it didn't sound like me.

He checked my blood pressure but didn't tell me what it was but that he thought it was due to my blood sugar and if I got it down the symptoms would most likely go away in a couple days. I had never had symptoms like this in my 30 plus years being a diabetic, but instead of questioning him I just hoped he was right. I told him I would go home and get it down myself instead of racking up another 5,000-dollar bill from the hospital. He wanted me to stay while they got my blood sugar down, but I said no.

My friend Matt had come up while I was there too. He was going to take me home and kept telling this doctor it was not my diabetes because I was all messed up and sounded funny. But the doctor didn't listen, so the nurse signed me out as refusing treatment or something and Matt and I left.

He dropped me off at the apartment and said to call him if I needed anything. Steve was there so he felt safe leaving. Now, my memory doesn't serve me well here, but Steve and I were supposed to leave for NASCAR weekend in Texas the next morning and I told Steve that the doctor said it was my blood sugar and the symptoms would go away.

I really wanted to go and see all my friends. This week had

been horrible, and I needed to get away. Steve said okay even though he tried to talk me out of going. I had called Mom to tell her what was happening to me and she said I sounded funny on the phone. I told her I thought it was a stroke, but the doctor said it was diabetes. She said to call Grandpa and ask him what Grandma's symptoms were when she had her strokes.

Grandpa said it sounded like a stroke and I should go to the hospital. I cried. I didn't want to think about it, I just wanted it to go away. By Friday I couldn't walk at all, I practically had to be carried, or I'd hold on to tables, desks, chairs, sofas, or people. But I was in serious denial at this point and went to Texas with Steve. Thinking that the doctor's diagnosis sounded better, and it would go away. Hoping that I'd wake up in the morning and it would all be better.

Everyone was really nice to me at NASCAR, but it wasn't fun. I felt isolated and lonely. I didn't know what was going on with my body, didn't want to go with everyone to party, felt tired, worn out, and like I was just a downer to Steve. The whole weekend was a blur, I didn't even go to the race because I couldn't walk. So, when I was alone, I just cried.

Steve and I left really early in the morning on Monday I think, it may have been Sunday. All my days are mashed together. Mom had called me and said she would be home Tuesday night and would take me to a free doctor on Wednesday. I had no insurance with my job and being diabetic no one would insure me.

By Wednesday it had been 8 days since this started. Mom took me to Catholic Charities early in the morning. I couldn't get in her car or even walk a step for that matter. She picked me up and threw me in her car. Then she held me up and tried to walk into the clinic. They came out quickly with a wheelchair and when we got inside the nurse gave Mom this pink slip of paper and said to go straight to St. Francis ER and to come in the Wednesday after I got out of the hospital. The pink slip basically said to treat me, and Catholic Charities would pay for everything.

Mom took me to the ER, and everything is kind of a blur, but it was so busy that there were people on the floor and on IV's in the waiting room because there were no beds. But I seemed to get in pretty quickly and then they took me to give me an MRI. They told me my blood pressure was high, no one had ever told me that before. We waited for the results of the MRI. They came back within like 30 minutes and the doctor said they were admitting me, that I had a massive stroke of the right brain stem. They still don't know what caused it. I told Mom to go ahead and leave and get Tori from school. I had to wait in ER for hours before getting a room. I fell asleep.

Stroke

I got a room sometime that evening. Steve was going to come up the next day and bring some things. Mom was coming up the next day too. I don't remember everything over the next several days so I will tell you the moments I do remember.

I remember Mike and Bobby coming to see me. Mike was my best friend, Bobby was a good friend of ours. They came together. Mike was using a cane but otherwise looked really good. They brought me flowers.

Mike said he was still waiting on a diagnosis about his leg and that he hurt a lot. But he smiled and made me feel better inside just by being there. He was always the first one to be there for me whenever anything was wrong.

I remember my Grandparents coming up and they brought me flowers too. I really love flowers. We talked for a while, but I can't really remember it. Everything was blurry or hazy in my mind from my stay in the hospital. Mostly I remember crying all the time, thinking way too much about what I was going to do now and seeing more and more doctors.

I couldn't walk, I couldn't move my left side at all. It felt like I was stuck in a small space and couldn't move. I slept a lot and every time I woke up I would think it was a dream and that I could move again. But then I would try and nothing happened. It was frustrating and irritating and I just wanted the use of my body again. I wanted to get out of bed, wanted to take a shower by myself, I wanted to get dressed by myself, brush my hair. I just wanted my life back.

Mom kept telling me that Steve was going to leave me. She had been telling me this ever since I called her when she was in Vegas. It made me cry and I told her he wouldn't, he seemed okay. How do you answer something like that? It wasn't in my control, I didn't tell myself to have a stroke, to make myself not work or walk or drive. Would he really leave me? Would I blame him?

I was in the hospital for eight long days. They were trying to get a bad for me in their rehab wing of the hospital but it was full. I asked them if they could send me home until there was room. They sent an occupational therapist and a physical therapist into my room to evaluate me and teach me some exercises to help me. They taught me how to use a walker and then said they were going to discharge me to my home. They would let me do in-home rehab and speech therapy instead of staying in the hospital. I was happy for this because I wanted to be home and be near Steve. I missed him while I was in the hospital and can't really describe how much I needed him to be there.

Mom drove me home from the hospital and Steve was pulling in at the same time we got there, so he helped Mom get me inside. It felt so good to be in my own apartment again. The hospital felt so cold and uninviting. Mom said bye and I gave her a kiss and she left.

I still sounded really funny when I talked, my speech was bad, and I hated it. I'm a talker and found myself trying to just be quiet so people couldn't hear me. I fell a lot too. I had absolutely no balance anymore. Even with the walker I lost my balance all the time, I could just be standing and would fall over.

I slept downstairs on the couch because I couldn't climb the stairs to the bedroom. I only got to shower once a week when Mom came over because I couldn't wash my hair myself while having to hold on to the wall with my one good arm to keep from falling. I didn't have a shower chair then; I didn't know all the things I would need or that were available to help me at that time.

My rehab therapists started coming out about a week after I got home, and I slowly got my speech back to normal using exercises the speech therapist gave me and talking a little slower and pronouncing myself better.

My physical therapist taught me how to climb stairs so that I wouldn't have to sleep on the couch every night. She also taught me how to go down the stairs backwards to put less pressure on my knees. I was happy for this because I missed sleeping in my bed and I missed sleeping next to Steve.

I was extremely emotional the first few weeks after my stroke but was told this was normal. I cried even if something was not sad. I would cry if I talked to anyone about anything. I couldn't control my emotions at all and I kind of got used to crying at least ten times a day.

I didn't talk on the phone anymore unless it was family or Mike. I still felt like I talked funny and if I started talking about my health or my recovery I would cry. So, I just didn't talk.

I felt really alone in my recovery. Everything was so difficult and took every ounce of energy I had to do even small things. I couldn't do our laundry anymore; I couldn't cook anymore, and I liked to cook for pleasure and because I liked doing it for Steve. I couldn't drive anymore and losing my ability to drive took away a huge part of my life. I couldn't go see my family, couldn't go see my friends, couldn't go to Steve's shows anymore or go pick up food. Depending on others to come see me doesn't happen. People mean well but while they say they will come see you or take you to dinner or just talk it never happens.

It doesn't mean they don't care about you or what you are going through, but their lives go on, they have work, bills to pay, shows to do, friends to hang out with. Life keeps going. This really made me feel alone. I tried to hide the sadness as much as I could because Mom said Steve would leave me if I cried all the time. I wish it were so simple.

I would sleep a lot during the day, it felt like I just couldn't get enough sleep. To seem okay I would wake up before Steve came home and try to smile when he was there. Still I felt things changing with him. I loved him with all of me. I gave him as much as I had to give but still felt he was pulling away, working more. I had no income at all since I couldn't work anymore. My

Grandpa said he would pay my portion of the rent and bills until I was approved for disability. Mom paid my cell phone bill and I received food stamps to help with my part of the food.

I became co-dependent on Steve. I needed him close to me all the time. I felt alone and sad if he was at work or out with friends or anywhere. I only felt better if he was there, encouraging me and motivating me to do better and keep up with rehab.

His Mom was really sick most of November of that year. It was terrible timing for Steve because not only was he having to do everything for me, do the laundry, cook dinner, clean house, shop and make sure everything was close to me when he left for work, but he also was very worried about his Mom who wasn't eating and was throwing up and not able to walk.

Thanksgiving came and Steve and I were going to my Aunt Sandra's house that afternoon. He was going to see his Mom at OSU Medical before we left to wish her and his Dad Happy Thanksgiving and see how she was doing. I stayed home because getting me out was hard enough and I also didn't want to take away from his Mom time or have his Dad make a fuss over me and if I was comfortable or needed anything when Judy was lying in a hospital bed not eating and looking so tiny.

Steve got home around noon and we left for Bartlesville. I don't remember much about Thanksgiving. My memory isn't so great anymore. I only remember my Uncle Steve telling Steve he was a good man and to take care of me.

Steve got a call at home a couple of days later, his Mom had passed. I think it was November 28, 2010. I cried. I felt so awful. He lost his Mom, his biggest fan. The pain he must have felt, I couldn't even imagine. I hugged him and he cried. He left for the hospital a few minutes later. November was a devastating time.

I had the anniversary of my rape the next day and I know that sounds weird, but it was a day that I knew every year, it was a dark day, it was always a cold day. I kept it to myself, Steve was in pain already.

It had been three or four weeks since my stroke and almost

two weeks since I got out of the hospital. I was still doing terrible and hated asking for help with anything. I liked being able to do things for myself and being in control of my own finances and work and free time. Since the stroke I had no sense of control over any part of my life or the choices being made for me.

Steve and I had gone to his Mom's house to get a few things and see his Dad. His Dad was always so sweet to me. I had only met him a couple times, but he always put my comfort above himself. A very warm man. We had already had the funeral for his Mom. It was a beautiful ceremony and she had beautiful flowers everywhere. There was a lot of love.

Steve and I got a few things from the house and he gave me her pill carrier and her blood pressure monitor. I still use both all the time. Then we left her home and drove back to Tulsa. We had been getting along fine. Steve never fought with me, I loved him too much to ever want to and we just seemed to get along.

When we got home, we were watching TV that night and Steve said something about after our year lease was up that he wanted to be single. I was taken by surprise because he had never said anything like this. So, I asked him if he wanted to break up and he said yes.

I don't remember much after that. I remember crying and constantly thinking it was over and here we were in this lease for a year. Mom was right and how would I live without my Steve. I wish I could answer that question, but I still can't to this day.

I never had a bad day with Steve before December of 2010. I never had an argument that meant I was going to leave him. Never had any man look at me and make me want to look at life without Steve.

I could lie to you, say Steve is a cheater, a liar, an abuser, and a thief. But it would be far from the truth. He's as close to perfect as I'll ever be. He never lied to me, he never cheated on me, he always cared for my heart and gave the best of himself to me. I don't know if any part of our relationship was real or true, maybe we were both living a big, fat lie and just didn't want to face it.

I went on after my stroke, in an unbelievably bad way. I dove headfirst into sorrow and pain. If there was a light, I never caught a glimpse of it. Every day was harder, more painful than the day before. The last piece of me that was left, broke in pieces on the floor after Steve left me.

I can't tell you how I felt, I could not breathe, I was drowning, suffocating, dying inside. I was done trying to make my life work or believing in anyone in mine. Promises broken, my soul was broken. Steve moved on easily. That hurt. Steve partied, dated, had fun, went to work, that hurt. I couldn't get away from any of it.

Then in one moment, he was gone, and he took all that love with him, and left me with this big, dark, empty pool with nothing but tears in it! So dark had my life become that I stopped seeing a way out. There was no light, no inspiring moment, his love was gone, never to be again. I thought with him there, I could still beat this. I would walk again, and I would fight to be better. But the night he broke up, was like a light crashing to the ground, left me in total darkness, nowhere to turn, nothing to see, I was a blank page in the dark with nothing to write. It was all gone for me.

I longed for my short days to end and my long nights to end and to feel some sort of safety & security in my life. It was cold when I went to bed, cried myself to sleep in silence with my ex-boyfriend asleep next to me, why, I'm not sure. We weren't together, not even in love, just torture to my heart to sleep beside a man who no longer cared. It left me longing for what we had in the year before this had happened left me lonelier than ever, unable to move on with the man, who I had given everything to, living in the same small space with me. Unable to date again or go meet someone new. I couldn't work, I couldn't drive, I could barely shower alone, dress myself, I didn't cook anymore, didn't care about any of it. The sky had fallen on me and I was suffocating.

I took a bunch of Amitriptyline one night, knowing it could kill me, because a friend of mine said his wife had committed suicide using that. I took the last 10 pills in my bottle and after an hour felt sleepy and dizzy and like I would pass out! I had called April and left her a message that I wanted any money I had to go to Kendall and that I was tired of everything. I prayed to God to please take me into heaven and away from this darkness and kept praying "the Lord is my God" and to please let me not wake up ... and went to bed crying myself to sleep. Steve woke me up some time during the night saying the police wanted to talk to me, I got up, but I was weak & dizzy, probably from the pills. They had been called by my sister, who had tried calling me, but I didn't answer. She called them from Las Vegas and told them she wanted them to come check on me. They talked to me & asked why I was dizzy & I said it was probably my blood pressure was too low, they checked it & it was 58 over 69 which was pretty low but I told them that was normal with my meds ... they asked if I was going to hurt myself & I said no. They left a few minutes later but gave me a number to call the next day.

I had no hope. None, no light in my life, nothing to look forward to but a broken body that wouldn't work and some bad memories. I slept all day and only woke up for a couple of hours at a time. I had no one to talk to and nothing to live for. Everything was just cold and dark and scary.

Steve had been what I thought was the love of my life, the perfect guy for me. Friends started telling me that they knew he was breaking up, but I just couldn't see it. I still can't see it. All I thought about that year living with him was what had I done wrong, why did he want to go? I had to swallow painful tears so many times. He was trying to date some girl named J'na from his work ... and I still hadn't found a way to stop hurting. That didn't work out for him, so he moved on to someone named Ashley. I don't know what happened with her.

The truth is, I couldn't let go. I lived with him the entire year, trying to get better but being pushed back down at every turn. I couldn't get any control over what I felt. Abandoned, isolated, pitied, and sad. Just so much intense pain. Steve went out to his shows or out with friends and stayed out late after work. I was utterly alone.

That's when I knew something had to change. I called the number the next day; it was a suicide prevention & Family and Children Services. I set up an appointment for help and went three days later to talk to someone. I needed someone to hear me, listen and hear the pain I felt that I could not get away from.

That same month our lease was up and another hurdle to jump over for me. My family packed my things for me and moved me in one day. I moved to an apartment in Tulsa by myself. Doctors were worried, Mom was really worried, and I was secretly terrified. Steve had moved out earlier that day and said a quick goodbye and I didn't see him again for a week or so.

Mike and I talked almost every night via Skype or Facebook video chat. He was sick. He understood the things I was going through because he was in a wheelchair now and getting ready to stop working so he could deal with his illness.

My friend Matt and his girlfriend, and my friend, Susan came by to see me in my new apartment one night. It was October 24, 2011. I remember because I was still crying constantly but I had started on a new anti-depressant and it was changing me for the better. I used to not get out of bed all day, or get dressed, or eat. This drug they put me on made me want to get up, get dressed, and write. It wasn't sudden but it was good and getting better.

Anyway, Matt and Susan came in carrying two pet carriers and these two little kittens were in them. One carrier was pink and the other was blue. These sweet little meows were coming from them and Matt opened the pink one up and out came this tiny little thing meowing and talking away and exploring my house. It took me less than two seconds to fall in love. Oh my gosh she was so sweet and fuzzy. She came right to me and Matt said Happy Birthday. She was mine! I named her right away, her name was Abby. I wanted to name my first daughter Abby, but I didn't get to have babies, so she was my baby.

I had a new reason to wake up in the morning, I had a reason to play. I got my first happy feeling in a year that day. It was truly the best feeling in the world. She went everywhere with me. I took her to Mom's when I visited her. She liked Mom's house. She liked to ride on my walker, and she fell asleep every night sucking on my earlobe and pawing my shoulder. Abby has been my light, my rock, my inspiration, and my friend every day since then.

This note is probably not placed in perfect order with my story, but the stroke made me feel trapped. Being unable to move or do anything with my left side felt like a prison that I was sentenced to for life. Having my job gone, my boyfriend no longer there for me, my friends unwilling to drive to my place to encourage me or talk to me felt very lonely.

2011

I felt a lot of loss when I moved into my own place, I was scared, I was angry, and I was frustrated. It took a lot to get the hang of living by myself. My friend, Mike, was my best friend and he couldn't drive anymore but we talked a lot on the phone and through video chats.

He had ALS and he understood my pains and frustrations with being disabled and being alone. He just got me, he was always there for me and trust me I had major breakdowns living alone. He always had such positive things to say, all the time, he was happy and smiling all the time, and he didn't ever give up on life or loving people, even though the disease he had was fatal and he knew he would progressively get worse.

Still, I could just tell him everything and he would never ever judge me for how I felt or what I did. We talked a lot about Steve. To be really honest I couldn't get over Steve. I had loved him completely, as much as a person can. I was angry with him, I still thought he left me at my lowest and most destructive point. I thought he left because I couldn't be "normal" anymore, I couldn't hang out at the bar anymore or go on camping trips. I thought because I couldn't pay for vacations and trips and going out now that I just wasn't any use to him.

Every word he ever spoke to me, every kiss, every look, every laugh and every promise, felt like just another lie and I wondered if the entire relationship that I thought was so perfect was really just one big lie. I was torn between the feelings that still held on strongly in my heart for Steve, what was really happening with him even though I didn't want to accept it and what he was telling me and promising me over what I was afraid the real truth of it all was.

Mike talked to me about these things. I think that I got some comfort from him because he said to me that Steve just couldn't handle such a huge loss from his Mom to me. It was just too much for him. I don't pretend to know if this is true, but it softened the blow to my emotional side.

Mike would tell me that anger is a bad thing to carry around and that I have no control of what others choose to do in a crisis. Mike always made so much sense. We did lots of crying and lots of laughing every time we talked, and we always ended our calls with an "I love you" and feeling more whole than either of us did without each other.

2011 was a year of transformation for me. I had gotten in touch with my friend, Adam, who I had grown up with. Actually, we had remained friends through all the years, he was one of those who I didn't see but we talked a lot and was a forever friend. I remember Adam so well.

He was such a beautiful soul. He had a mesmerizing smile and sparkling eyes and tan skin and was like this handsome man. I can't even explain how handsome Adam was. He was tormented by things through the years. He worried about his Mom and her health, he had lost his Dad already. His Mom ... he loved her to the moon and back.

He had been in some bad relationships. But he had been in a good relationship with some girl named Beth because he used to talk about going to shows with Beth, or going out with Beth, or cooking dinner at her house, or he was talking about his dog or cat. Adam was an animal lover, always sweet and caring. He was just a warm and inviting person.

Truthfully, Adam was insanely beautiful from his smile to his sparkling eyes to his hair to his skin color he was just breathtaking and from the time we were young I had always loved him more than I ever said. I didn't tell him about my feelings because I never deserved him, and I didn't want to lose the friendship because I couldn't keep my feelings to myself.

Adam had called one night and had concerns about needing a new job. I talked to Steve about getting him a job where he was a kitchen manager, so I told Adam to go apply and ask for Kim and put Steve down as a reference.

So, he got hired there and called to thank me, he was so happy. I was happy to help him because I loved Adam. Then sometime in December about Christmas or the day before or after he moved into a new apartment. He was excited for the changes he was making, but still said he needed to change his relationship. I think he was having a hard time because Adam never wanted to hurt others and kind of ran away from issues that would hurt someone.

Then Christmas he left a voicemail saying Merry Christmas and to tell my Mom the same and he loved me. That was the last time I heard Adam's voice. There was a fire on the 29th I believe it was. Something electrical sparked and Adam was asleep. He woke up to his then girlfriend and daughter telling him to get out of the apartment. They made it out, but Adam didn't, and they said he was trying to save his animals.

His ex-girlfriend Beth had messaged me or called me, I know I spoke to her on the phone and she told me he had died in the fire. I was in shock at first, he couldn't have died, he had just called me on Christmas. But the way she cried, I knew it was true. I lost it.

He was only a year older than me. He was so happy about turning his life around. Things were looking up for him. He was such a good friend; Adam and I had a crush on each other as kids, but we never explored that because we didn't want to lose what we had.

Honestly, I just cried and called my Mom. Then sat on my couch and cried some more. I just kept thinking I was supposed to die before my friend. I was sick, had a stroke, had been raped, had a coma, why was I still alive and he wasn't? I hurt so bad inside and I was an emotional blob anyway with my life. I don't think even now I will ever understand how some continue to live while others die. And sometimes I am jealous that they are gone, and I am not.

I wish I had more conversations with him. I used to listen to his voice on my voicemail or call his phone just to hear it. He had a warm, soft voice. I kept thinking that I hope he didn't have pain or suffer.

I became friends with Beth after he passed. We gave each other strength and could think about our good memories of him. He never showed up for work, and I told Steve he wouldn't be because he died. I lost one of my closest friends that day and I don't think you can console that kind of devastation.

I kind of opened my heart a little more after Adam passed, chose to put my anger aside and became friends with Steve. He was really there for me, not just now, but through a lot of changes in my life, a lot of really devastating times and a lot of bitterness.

I could talk about all my resentment all day long, but it wouldn't change the fact that Steve wanted to be part of my life. He was encouraging, he completely surprised me. When we dated, I really thought he loved me, but I learned after we broke up that our love was meant for friendship.

Steve was a good soul. He genuinely cared, the things that sound negative about him, are just my perception of him at that time. It wasn't who he was, it was who I was. It was my anger, my jaded mistrust of him, my pain. It was the cold me trying to put up a wall between him and I.

After Adam passed so suddenly, death became much more unpredictable to me. There wasn't time to waste on being angry or wanting him to hurt the way I did. Life flies by, ends without warning and we live once, just once, so we have to think about what we want in our life.

Funny how something so tragic like losing a childhood friend can affect my entire life in a better way. Steve was awfully close to me; he saw things I'd never share with anyone. Seriously he lived that first year working so many hours at work, shopping, cooking, doing laundry, and trying to deal with his own loss. That loss was much greater than I could imagine and still he maintained it all so well.

He never broke down, well maybe a few times, but silently.

He dealt with my single worst year trudging through this swamp of dark feelings. I was so terrible then I am afraid of ever feeling what I felt then. He saw more of that then anyone else did and he really should have run. Why he even stayed and tried to help me I'll never know. He said once he should have ran when he had the chance. I can't blame him one little bit for leaving me, I was a wreck to myself and others.

Adam died at the end of 2011. That next year would prove to be just as hard for me on an emotional level. I felt no relief from my pain. The anti-depressant just made me feel locked in a box choking on my suffering. I didn't want to kill myself, but I didn't want to try anymore either. If I had to live this life for the rest of my life well then, I just didn't want to live it. I felt like my choices had been taken from me and what was left was just cold and nasty.

2012

At the end of 2011 I went with Mike to see AWOLNATION, a band I really love, he had bought tickets for us for our birthdays. That was an amazing concert at Brady Theater. Especially because Mike and I didn't see each other in person very often since neither of us could drive. Mike was in an electric wheelchair now because of his disease.

Mike was my best, best friend. He talked to me as no one else ever could, got me to open up about things I was afraid of and just got me. I love Mike the same way I love music, deeply, honestly, undeniably and in a way that I could never even try to explain to another person.

I got him into liking AWOLNATION as much as I did, and he got me hooked on Shinedown. I felt bad for Mike, always listening to my troubles and insecurities and how I was trying to get better with rehab and life since my stroke. He was getting more immobile but still feeling ok. He couldn't eat with his hand very well and his neck couldn't hold his head up very well. He couldn't walk or drive now. But his outlook on life was something I wanted.

Mike really helped me to stay sane being disabled and unable to do so many things that a young person does. I really missed doing those things, I missed hanging out with friends. I missed the things that Steve and I used to do together before my stroke.

I had a lot of anger towards Steve, it just felt better to have angry love then to have depressed love for him. I had grown so sick of my tears, so tired of feeling abandoned, and having no choice in whether that relationship could be saved or if it was just done.

Mike talked to me so many nights for hours about my heartache, which I still had after two years. Too afraid of what other people, family, friends would think if I spoke about it. I should have been done with that heartache long ago. But it lingered. I still felt love for him, still remembered how great I thought it was before the stroke. And I still felt this immense frustration and anger and unsettled feeling inside me.

I still hated seeing him date or tell me about his dates or telling me about going to the bar with 20-year-old kids. I couldn't do those things. I guess I felt like if I couldn't do it then he couldn't either because it wasn't fair. Selfish and nasty way to think I know. I couldn't think of anyone but Steve, I cried thinking how easy it would have been if I hadn't had the stroke and he left me. I could have filled the void, the emptiness with going out, meeting new people, working, finding someone else who would love me the right way.

As it was, I couldn't meet anyone, go anywhere, see friends, work with people, and be social. My life really took a drastic turn from very social and happy to having no visitors and no life at all. Mike didn't bring me out of that feeling, he just gave me hope for something better. He would always keep my secrets. He just completely understood me like no other person has ever understood me.

He had also gone from very social to having very few visitors. It's absolutely true what they say, if you want to know who is really in your life go through something horrible and see who sticks around. It's really not enough to say you will visit, or go to dinner or go out but never show up. Not even once.

But I hurt inside for Mike. I hated to know about his pain being so horrible. They had him on all kinds of medicine in 2012. Things that would help him sleep, pain pills, pains that helped him eat, helped the depression he was going through. Just so many things they had him on. And he still stayed up late at night and couldn't sleep.

He couldn't sleep in his bed anymore, he changed to a hospital bed and that helped. He said transferring him from his wheelchair was terrible. He had home nurses to bathe him, help him check his blood pressure, heart, breathing, swallowing and to do some therapy with his body.

I felt bad that I was getting somewhat better, at least able to live alone, bathe, eat and dress myself. At the same time, he had lost his ability to do these things. I felt guilty. I wanted to be encouraging and say things would get better, but that would just be a lie. He wouldn't get better; he could only get worse.

He had to move into a nursing home sometime in mid-2012. They just couldn't take care of him and watch him 24 hours a day like he needed. He couldn't risk a fall or choking on food. He needed more care. I cried when he had to go, can you imagine being almost 40 and having to go to a home? He had concrete walls and medical equipment and no family or friends there with him. They visited him often but just the thought of having to go to sleep in this place that felt cold and smelled of sickness and felt like a hospital.

I'm sorry this skips around a bit, my memory works in bits and pieces these days, one of the fun things about a stroke. Steve came over once a week to do laundry and hang out for a couple hours. He did this every week. I guess it was only through persistence and kept promises that we remained friends. He confused me, because I really thought he left because of my stroke, yet he seemed to really want to help me get better and be a friend. While it made me happy, it also made me sad because I thought he must have left because he just fell out of love. But then when did he fall out of love, did he allow me to move to Tulsa with him knowing he was going to leave? I felt sick with that thought.

He says he made a promise that he would not leave me and never see me. So he was keeping that promise. Sounds sweet doesn't it? But the way my mind works tells me that he only comes because I asked him to and not because he wants to. And no matter how I feel, I never want someone around who doesn't choose to be there for themselves, so now I just feel I am holding him to a promise that is unfair.

I also dated someone for about 8 months in 2012. He was

someone I knew through one of my close friends in grade school. I liked him many, many years ago and we just accidentally started seeing each other. He took my mind off of Steve. He made it hurt less. He seemed to be completely ok with my disability. Mostly he took me places and came over a lot and I needed that. He filled a void that needed to be filled. I don't say much about him because he left one night after spending a few hours with me and then just stopped calling, texting, deleted me and blocked me on Facebook and disappeared. It would have done me no good to question why he did that. Any answer would not have made it any easier or given me closure, I just allowed myself to hurt for a while.

During all of this, just life going on through 2012. But Mike was just getting worse. I felt like the helpless friend. We stayed close through our video chats and still talked almost every day. Mike always called me his butterfly which made me smile. Always the sweetest guy I knew. In November of 2012 he got sick and we would talk still but only for maybe half an hour. He would need to lay down and sleep and he couldn't get over this flu or cold he had.

It lasted almost 4 weeks, just feeling sick and his chest hurt, and he said it felt like strep or bronchitis, but he wasn't sure. I was worried and always encouraged him to rest more and let me know how he was. I also emailed his sister-in-law, Chelle, in November. I said something like to please call me right away, night or day, if Mike got worse or was in the hospital ... or died. It sounds bad to say that, but I knew this disease would eventually take his life and I promised Mike he would never be alone when he passed, that I would be there. I promised him. I meant it, I was not going to let him be afraid of being alone, which was a huge thing for him. He cried a lot saying he was lonely and didn't want to be alone. I guess it was just the one thing I could do for him.

It was right after his birthday in December, around the 4th or 6th I think when the nursing home sent Mike to the hospital. He had gotten worse and the hospital said he had pneumonia.

Chelle called me to tell me and I thought that was all and I was going to find a ride to the hospital. Chelle said the doctors said everyone should come see him because he was really bad, and they didn't know if he was going to make it. So, I called Mom, but she was in Tulsa and couldn't pick me up for several hours and I wanted to be right by his side right then. I didn't want to wait hours. So, I called Don and asked if he could please give me a ride to the hospital and he said yes.

I got there about an hour or so after Chelle had called. I had to walk a long way to get to the right elevators to his floor. I finally got there and started looking for Mike's room. I passed the nurses station and his room was right in front of it. But they said I couldn't see him yet because the doctor was there and I could go in in a few minutes, but that the rest of his family was down the hall on the right, so I went to find David & Chelle.

I finally found them in a small waiting room with a friend of Mike's. I can't remember who she was, but I think she was one of his home nurses. Then Chelle said hi and I said hi. Then she said Mike died ten minutes ago. I just started crying, like uncontrollable crying. I tried to hold it in, but I just couldn't. She said the doctor thought he had a stroke in his sleep and never woke up. All I kept thinking was that I wasn't with him. I was probably in the hospital, but I walk so slow since my stroke that I didn't make it to him. I felt so much pain in not being able to keep my promise. I couldn't believe my best friend was gone. Like he was gone forever. I couldn't video chat anymore or talk for hours or hug him or hear him laugh or give me advice. He couldn't do any of that anymore.

I had called Bobby, one of our other friends since high school. He was on his way to the hospital but hadn't made it yet. He got there about ten minutes after Chelle had told me about Mike. I remember he was smiling and wanted to go see Mike too. I had to tell him Mike died, and I don't think I've ever had to give someone such horrible news ever. I cried as I told him, and he was just like asking if I was serious. Then he hugged me. Then a nurse said we could go see Mike, that he was ready.

Bobby went with me to see him. Mike looked like he was sleeping. He didn't look dead. He looked peaceful. But I just knew he was gone because he always smiled so big when he saw me and wanted a hug, and this time he didn't do either of those things.

I think that's the day I gave up on God, not because the possibility of him wasn't there for me, but because I decided if he would put a disease like ALS into the body of a man who meant so much to so many, who had lived true and inspired every person who met him. If he could be so evil, then I no longer wanted to associate myself with him.

Mike would be mad at me for that, but I won't change my mind. Mike was one of the best people to ever be in my life and he shouldn't have gone so young. Thinking back on that day makes me break down. I called and told Mom and she said she was sorry, and she would go to his funeral with me.

Mike had donated his body for ALS research, so we had his picture at his funeral. Funeral is a heavy word, so his celebration of life and a time to share memories. They played Mike's favorite songs, AWOLNATION Sail, which was his first favorite song of theirs, the first one I played for him. And then they played our song The Crow and the Butterfly by Shinedown.

Mike always called me his butterfly and said this would be our song. And they played another one, but I can't remember. Friends & family got up and told memories of Mike or things they did together, but I cried too much to stand or tell any stories. Where would I begin? Mike was the chicken and I was the clown at Hardee's, that's how we first met, at our first job. Mike and I had way too many memories to even begin to talk about them.

After the service Chelle gave me his painting of this cross that he had designed, and that Mom had painted for him for his room at the nursing home. Shauna and Mom went to the service for Mike with me, he knew my whole family and they all loved Mike.

Now I have his painting hanging on my living room wall

where I can see it every day and think of him. Next to it on my entertainment center is a picture of Adam. Two people who died way, way too young and in terrible ways. I miss them both every day.

I still don't think I can make you understand the immense ache inside that I have for my friend. I don't think that I can go on without either of them here, because life had purpose and I had a place with them, and when they just aren't there in your everyday anymore, everything changes.

2013 – 2014

Several years in a row had proven to be life changing for me. I am not the only person to have things happen in my life. Life doesn't pick and choose. For me it was a divorce the first year, meeting Steve the next, having a stroke the next, losing Steve the same year, then the next year losing Adam and the following year losing my Mike.

To lie and say I handled it pretty well would just be stupid. I didn't. I handled everything horribly. It felt like being pushed underwater and fighting for one breath and then being pushed back under, and doing this continually for several years. I ended up toxic to myself and anybody who came close to me.

I shut down for the most part. I promise there was a time when I was sweet and fun and beautiful. Seems like a million years ago. In 2013 I had a stronger friendship with Steve, having lost my best friend in the world, Steve really filled a huge void in my life. He texted me every night and came by one day every week and brought me dinner and lottery tickets. He didn't really ever leave me, he just changed our relationship from an intimate, personal one to one that just had a tremendous amount of love between friends.

Don had left in early November of 2012 and I had a lot of sadness over that one. Steve got me through it. He is straight to the point, no frills, but supportive. He'd tell me I was going to be fine and to write or do something or chill out. Steve liked to tell me to chill out.

What I'm getting at here is that Steve became my best friend. After I put away my own selfish feelings and thought about his own struggles and his own loss I was able to love him again in a better way. He seriously never really talked about how he felt or how he handled things in his own life. And I feel really sick for not being able to see his own issues with everything.

The rest of 2013 was really the most uneventful year I had in quite some time and I was really happy for that. I was getting used to being alone a lot, settling in to my awkward way of walking, and felt good. My sister, Shauna, was having a baby in May of 2014 so I got to watch her tummy grow. She got engaged on Christmas to a really sweet man and had graduated college and was teaching.

I spent a lot of time at the end of 2013 working on my 20-year reunion with a few other girls. It kept me busy and kept my mind on things besides the loss of Mike. I got lucky when they had asked me to help plan this reunion. And I really wanted to get in contact with as many classmates as I could and just put my heart and soul into making it great.

Kendall came out and spent the summer with me every year and then spent two weeks at Christmas. I think those are always my best months. She's just this amazing kid. I don't know how we ended up with such a brilliant kid. She is always so helpful, so full of life, so happy to be here. I secretly think maybe I had a little bit to do with who she is, and it makes me really proud.

I came to terms with where I stood with life now. Things don't go as we plan, we just have to be willing to change with the circumstance. I knew I would never have kids of my own now, I also know that I will probably never get married again and maybe I won't even find a man in this life.

I still see doctors all the time. Four years now since my stroke and I have a laundry list of medications that are supposed to keep me healthy and I don't know if they will. Most of the side effects are what's the worst part. They make me tired, numb, dizzy, have night sweats, nauseas. I have headaches and body aches and even with all the medicine I still get those electrical currents through my left side and every muscle tightens up on me. I suppose there is no cure for everything.

I think there is a lot of help out there for stroke victims, as far as rehabilitation, therapy, doctors, and equipment. They make everything you could need as a handicapped person. The one thing they don't have enough of is support for the emotional loss, the loss of independence. The side of it that you don't see. There's a struggle every day to just be content with what life is for me now. They need far more support for the sudden loss of a life in every aspect. Your world changes in one moment, everything. It's not some slow transitioning into a slower life, it's like a huge thunderstorm just barrels down on you in an instant.

This year I had my 20-year reunion in September, and it was so much more than I ever thought the four of us girls could put together. I saw so many faces, so many friends that will always be a special part of my life. Everyone had a great time, April even got to fly from Las Vegas and come. I took Mom and my Aunt Sandra with me and we had an amazing night.

So, things do go well. It's all a give and take. I guess I've learned to be more open minded about my world, to love every day without fail and to say "I love you" often because you just don't know what will happen next. I have a quote from a song by AWOLNATION called Kill Your Heroes, and it says "Never let your fear decide your fate". I live by this every day.

I don't hold back anymore. If I have an opinion or I feel a certain way I say it. I won't allow myself to stay quiet to appease others. Not to say there isn't a respect and kindness towards everyone. But instead of living through a boyfriend or a husband and losing myself in the process, I will live for me now. I make my choices; I take responsibility for them.

Life has many, many roads. It's not like they always say where there's a road that twists and turns or there's one that is straight and narrow. No, I have learned that there are many roads in each of our lives. And I don't know if we always make a conscious decision to take the short narrow one or to take that wide and winding one. I think that certain trials come upon us and make all the difference in where we go.

I've thought so much about whether I would choose the easy life. Would I be happier if I had gone a different way? Do I need the challenges and the pain that will surely come by taking that road that turns at the corner and has rocks that I must move or stumble over?

I have chosen the one that leads me to troubles and to sorrow and to pain, and somehow, I have found along this path so much joy and love and compassion. I have been weak and frail and lonely so many times, and yet I have also grown stronger by these trials. I have seen things that I never knew before. Things that many people may never see or feel.

Sometimes I feel like maybe I have cheated death. I wonder what my purpose must be. Always I know that I do have some purpose here, although I do not know what it is. I have been lucky, well many call it luck. I know the fear of death. The fear of losing someone or something that you cannot live without. I know the pain of losing myself and being dependent upon another. I remember the deep longing and uncertainty of what tomorrow would bring to me. Would I always feel useless? Would I look into that mirror one day and smile, loving that person who looks back at me?

But through all of it, I somehow found hope. The flame that burns inside of me that I didn't know was there. Such a tiny spark, dim and weak, but there all the same. And through every trouble I had to see through, there it was, burning strong.

I found my reason to be alive. I changed my life. It isn't perfect and I still fight every day against the demons that surround me, but they will always be there. I choose to be responsible for everything that happens to me, for every choice I make and every lesson I learn

I could either live or die. I choose to look at my entire life and allow every moment that I've had, good or bad, teach me something. Maybe it would make me wiser, maybe it would make me a little smarter, or maybe it would allow me to reach out with compassion.

I know I had a point to all of this. I see my life and it amazes me. I don't consider myself better than anyone else. I sometimes just can't believe that I am here. But I have gained so much from this life. Though the trials were uncommonly difficult, I have found such peace inside.

From my rape, I learned how to talk and to understand. I found strength where I never knew it existed. I learned how to cry and to feel pain. I also learned compassion for others and a love for helping others that I didn't know was in me. I learned who my friends were and what it was to be a friend. I figured out that I didn't need to have all the answers or give advice that all that I needed was to listen and to say I would be there no matter what.

I understood what true love for my family was. I finally knew why I needed them and why they were the most important people in my life, because they loved me, and they stood beside me and they would never give up on me. They shared my pain and I felt theirs. I hurt to know they hurt but I also felt closeness in sharing with them and knowing they understood.

Through my coma I realized you need patience. That I wanted something so much that I couldn't have until the time was right. I learned that I couldn't have everything. I had to feel the ache of wanting my loved ones there. I had to understand that something had to change. I had to stop hurting the ones I loved. By giving up I would hurt so many people.

And from my car wreck, I experienced for a short time how it feels to be handicapped. How people stare and laugh at you sometimes. I also learned that even in the weakest people there is an undying strength and will to be well again. To never give up on what I could do. I realized how I escaped death three times, at least, and that I was blessed. That life was never to be perfect. Life brings upon us many trials, which only make us stronger.

My life is tough. Everyone has tough times. I have realized that all the times I thought I was being cheated; I should be thankful for. I know that if I feel lonely and I feel like I can't go on, I have to break down those bars. For the prison I am in, I make myself. No stranger can rape me and take my life away. No self-pity can take the place of my love for family and their love for me. And no car wreck can make me give up on life.

It's ok to be vulnerable. It isn't a character flaw. Being vulnerable gives me honesty and love. It makes me real and open, and these are things some search for their entire life. A smile is such a beautiful thing. I love the girl in the mirror because she's still here and because she will never give up no matter how hard it gets. One day I'll get there, to that place I need to be. For now, I love, I laugh, and I have hope.

Sure, the girl I see in the mirror is getting older and I really don't like that, but I love it! I love it because every birthday I celebrate, from here until I'm gone, is another year of life. Another chance to meet someone knew, maybe a chance to be married. Maybe or maybe not.

2015 – 2016

This is my final chapter, not to say there won't be years to come in my life, though you never know. This year hasn't been a wonderous, beautiful year but it hasn't been life taking either. I got a Gastric Pacemaker this year for my Gastroparesis. In time, my hope is to be able to eat like an ordinary person. I was on a liquid diet for nearly a year and any time I attempted eating real food I would be in excruciating pain, throw up for days and end up worse off.

So far since getting the pacemaker in February of 2016 it has been up and down, but my weight has been steady, and I am no longer malnourished.

I'm not going to lie; I still wish things were different. I wish I weren't here at all. I wish Mike was here, Adam was here, Steve loved me, friends didn't walk away without a word, the stroke had never happened, work was possible, I could drive a car again, I could hold my new baby nephew. But we all wish for things that we just can't have, and we cannot spend all our time asking why we can't have those things.

The point to it all is to keep going, push forward, fight like it's all you have, don't deny your feelings, or allow anyone to make them seem worthless. Make the most of what you can do and forget about what you can't do. Live and love yourself, even if no one else can love you, remember that is not your problem anymore.

Stroke

This is days before and during and days after the stroke.

I was dating Steve since August of 2009, and in October of 2010 he wanted us to get a place in Tulsa that would be closer to both of our jobs. We had been living at my apartment at The Greens in Owasso before this. We moved into our 2-bedroom apartment on October 28th, 2010, 2 days before my 35th birthday.

Steve had to move EVERYTHING without me there to help because I had to work. But he said he could get it done; I had packed everything up really well already. So, when I got home from work around 5:30 I was tired and had an awful headache, and I should add, I never get headaches. My chest also felt tight. I figured it was from being tired from the packing, long day at work, and my Gastroparesis acting up again.

I could barely get the door opened and squeeze inside. Steve had gotten everything unloaded and taken the truck back, but everything was in the living room and dining room, so you couldn't quite find the furniture cause of all the boxes. I think back, and I'm not that girl who gets mad and is mean to people. Steve and I never even fought ever. But feeling the way I did and not being able to walk or sit anywhere, I started crying.

I said something to Steve about how you couldn't even get to the stairs or walk across the room, which was horrible on my part. First thing I needed to say was that he did a great job all by himself and thank you. I knew he was mad cause he said nothing and went upstairs to put the bed together.

The next morning was Friday, I woke up feeling better that morning, less stress and I only hoped Steve was not still mad at me. I didn't want to wake him up since he worked at 4pm so I'd have to ask him later. I was still a bit scared about moving to Tulsa, living with Steve, and having to depend on him for things since it was me and him. I just didn't want things to go wrong, but bad luck seems to follow me around. I had asked him a couple times if he was positive, he wanted to move in with me because if he wasn't, I would just sign another lease in Owasso. I just knew he had been a bachelor for a long time and liked being on his own, at least before we met. But he said that we should do it and Steve never lies ... which is one of the best things about him.

OK, so I went to work Friday, and it was boring that day, just a bunch of numbers, bills, A/R and A/P. My headache came back before lunch and I thought maybe it's allergies. I bought some Excedrin Migraine on my way home from work. Steve was at work when I got home, so I moved things, unpacked boxes, and went to bed. Saturday the 30th (my birthday) I pretty much did the same thing until about 3pm.

Freaker's Ball was Saturday night at Cain's Ballroom and Steve, Dave, Rich, and Alex were one of the bands playing. It was also a costume thing for Halloween. I still had this pretty aggressive headache but just took another pill and didn't really have time to think about it. I had to get Steve ready and then myself, he was going to be a Werewolf and I was a Candy Corn Witch (because I save costumes for years).

We got to Cain's with the rest of the band and my good friend, Matt, met me there to keep me company. I kept feeling dizzy and light headed during the event, but I guess I am good at not letting things show and I wasn't going to say anything because I wanted the guys to feel good and not be worried about me.

I did tell Matt that I needed to go sit down for a minute, so he walked with me to the seats and then he went to wait in line for the bathroom. All I really remember is feeling like I might pass out, my head throbbing and feeling nauseous. I sat there for 10 minutes or so until Matt got back and then we went to find the guys, who had finished their set, and we all hung out until late listening to some of the other bands and watching Dave's son, Ethan, win the costume contest ... he was Chuckie. I think we went straight to bed when we got home.

Sunday was Halloween, and two of Steve's friends were getting married, so we had to dress up for the wedding, Steve was a zombie and I just wore my witch costume again. I don't consider myself super social, but I am comfortable talking to anybody, and I met lots of people Steve worked with and had fun. I don't think we did anything after the wedding but go home and shower and go to bed. I had to work the next day, on November 1st.

I forgot to mention that I had not been eating for a couple of days because I threw up any time I ate. It was likely the Gastroparesis. I also still had the annoying headache, which was horrible since I don't typically ever get headaches and this one had gone on for nearly a week. I went to work and hoped this gross feeling would go away soon. Monday was Monday, I was tired, and the day took forever.

Tuesday was November 2nd, 2010 and I woke up to my alarm clock at 6:30am. Steve was asleep in bed; he always fell asleep in like 2 minutes and never woke up. But he had to work later so I was quiet. I got dressed and then went to the bathroom to brush my teeth and my hair. I always put my makeup on in my car in the parking lot at work. I'm not sure why, that's just what I did.

I was getting ready to walk downstairs to grab my phone and car keys and suddenly felt hot and sick and dizzy. I took the first step down the stairs and my legs just seemed to crumble under me and I ended up loudly sliding down the entire staircase to the bottom step. I sat there for a couple minutes trying to figure out what happened and collect myself, then I started to laugh and hoped I hadn't woken Steve up. I was glad no one saw me do that!

My left foot hurt but I grabbed my shoes and put them on, got my keys and went to work. I stopped at QT and got my coffee before going around the corner to work at the law firm. I opened the office, turned the lights on, the computers, machines, set up our sitting area and made coffee. I set up the conference room for the attorneys who had a meeting that day.

Jamie came in first, she was a Legal Secretary, and I loved her. I told her about my fall that morning and that my left foot was hurting but no one saw. Then I told her I was going to the courthouse about 3:00 so if she needed me to give anything to the judges or file anything to try to have it ready by then.

By the end of that workday my foot and ankle were swollen badly and hurt. But I handle pain very well, so I didn't let it slow me down. I got home about 5:30 and Steve was at work. I took a shower, ate dinner, and watched TV until he got home later that night. We stayed up until about 2am and went to bed.

I got up for work Wednesday morning and my foot was worse and I still felt very lightheaded but went to work hoping it would start going away. My ankle looked bad, mostly from the swelling, it was 3 times the size of my right ankle. I also noticed I was limping, and it was noticeable. Jamie asked me about it, and I told her if it didn't get better, I would see a doctor.

Around mid-afternoon, I was in the supply room making copies and faxing things and the phone rang. I picked up the phone in the supply room and then tried our company's name, but all these weird words came out. I tried again and still it came out all wrong. Jamie came in to copy something and I stared at her blankly and tried to say, "help me" and it came out very slurred like if I was really drunk. She came running and I got really dizzy and my legs gave out on me again, she picked me up and grabbed a chair and sat me down and gave me coke. A few minutes later I felt fine, I was talking very normal and couldn't figure out why that happened.

I was fine the rest of the day and the only issue was my foot hurt horribly. I finished work and drove straight home to clean house and do laundry. Steve was at work already, he worked almost every day but typically from about 4pm to midnight. I gathered up all the laundry, there was a lot since we had moved. I walked down to the apartment laundry room which was across the courtyard and down in the basement of the main building.

I put all the laundry in and waited for all of it to wash before leaving. I figured I'd leave while it was drying since that took about 45 minutes. Finally, I got it into the dryers, we had three loads since we had clothes needing to be washed from before and after the move. I walked up the stairs and across the courtyard to our apartment, but I noticed sharp, electric shocks going through my left side that literally made me stop walking several times. My limp on my left leg was also more like dragging instead of limping. I could barely even lift my leg.

I went inside and laid on the couch with my left leg elevated thinking that might help. I watched TV for about 45 minutes and then slowly walked back to the laundry room. I put all the clothes in my tall clothes hamper so I could fold or hang them at home. I tried to carry the hamper but, for some reason, it kept falling out of my hand. I could not keep hold of it and couldn't grip it with my left hand. So, I dragged it across the laundry room to the stairs with my right hand and was fine.

My left hand felt weak, but I managed to grab the hamper with my left hand and hold the handrail with my right hand, but it was difficult for me to climb the stairs. It took me about 20 minutes to get up the 10 stairs. My left leg was just dragging now, and I could not walk with it at all. I started crying, I was alone, it was dark outside, and it took me at least 30 minutes, because I had to drag the hamper with my right hand and try to walk without my left leg. This is scary because I was able to easily carry the hamper to the laundry room, get down the stairs and use my hand before. So, all of this happened quickly.

I finally made it into the apartment, and I was out of breath and exhausted, my leg was hurting badly, and these electric shocks kept coming every couple of minutes. So, I just went and sat down for a few minutes without even trying to take the laundry upstairs. The tightening, tremors in my left leg and foot were irritating and hurt, and I had to keep moving my body to try and stop them because they were worse if they were still or not moving. My foot did have bruising, but it didn't look broken to me, but maybe it was.

Steve got home around 11 that night, and I hadn't told him about anything that happened at work. He knew I had fallen down the stairs getting ready for work though. I told him about the laundry and how I had a hard time with it. My foot was throbbing, probably from walking on it too much I assumed. I felt terrible and I could not get the tremors or shocks to go away. He was worried and kept asking if he needed to take me to ER. Finally, I said yes so, they could look at my foot.

This was November 3rd, the day after I had fallen down the stairs. The hospital took my blood sugar first thing, which is usual for a diabetic. It tested fine at 128, which was kind of shocking because in 2010 I did not regularly test my blood since I had no health insurance and back then being a Type 1 diabetic is a pre-existing condition and they would automatically refuse to cover you unless it was through your job. The hospital took me in for an X-ray on my foot to see if it was broken or anything. It took them a couple hours and I was impatient waiting in the room. I couldn't lie down because those electric shocks were terrible if I did, so I got up and walked around to make them better. The doctor came in and told us that my foot was not broken, but that it was probably a sprain with the bruising and swelling. So, I said ok and thank you and told Steve I just wanted to go home. The doctor said the nurse would be in soon to let me go. We were in that room for another hour, but no nurse came in. When the nurse finally did come in, she knew nothing, so I told her the doctor said it was not broken so I just wanted to go home if it was fine. She let us go.

Steve drove home and we stayed up for a few minutes and went to bed. It was late, and I had to wake up at 6:30am. Thursday morning, I went to work, but I felt awful and hurt badly. Jamie noticed it as soon as she came in and told me something is wrong. I couldn't walk without holding on to things and my speech was slurred and sounded weird. Some people couldn't tell my speech was off but knowing what I sound like and how I talk, I knew this was not normal. Jamie called an ambulance and said it could be Bell's Palsy, which I did not know about.

This little Asian man was my doctor at St. John's in the emergency room that morning. I told him that my speech was slurred and about my foot and leg on the left side. I told him about falling down the stairs on Tuesday and that I thought it may be a stroke, and that Jamie said it may also be Bell's Palsy. He kind of laughed and said I was too young to have a stroke. Then he tested my blood sugar, and it was near 200. It had been going up since Tuesday because I did not feel well. He said my speech sounded fine and he could understand me, and I told him it did not sound like I sound normally.

He checked my blood pressure but never told me what it was, I assumed it was fine or he would have said something. I should be clear here; he never did any tests on my brain or scans either. Today, I think it was because I did not have insurance, so he wanted to get me out of there. But he said he thought it was just because my blood sugar was a little high and if I could get it down, the symptoms would go away in a couple of days. I have been a diabetic for 30 plus years and had NEVER had symptoms like this for high blood sugar. But I did not question him, because he was the doctor and I, honestly, hoped that he was right, and I was wrong. I told him I would go home and get it down myself instead of getting another $10,000 bill from the hospital for an insulin IV.

He wanted me to stay until they got it down, but I said no, I have insulin at home and could do that myself. Matt was with me now because he had come up when I called him and told him. He kept telling the doctor it was not my blood sugar because I could barely walk or talk. But the doctor didn't want to listen, so the nurse signed me out "against medical advice" and Matt helped me to his car.

Matt took me to my apartment, got me inside, and said to call him if I needed anything at all. Steve was still home so Matt felt safe leaving me with him. Steve drove me to my work later that day, so I could drive my car home. We were supposed to go to

Texas Motor Speedway the next morning for NASCAR to meet up with about 15 of our friends. I was already off work and Steve was too since it was a 5-hour drive to get there. I told Steve we should still go because the doctor said just to get my blood sugar down and I would be fine. At that point, I was not wanting to accept how bad I was.

It had been an awful week for me, and I just wanted to go and see my friends and get away. Steve agreed we could go, though he was still really concerned. I had called Mom and told her what was happening, and she said I sounded funny. I told her that I really thought it was a stroke but had been to ER twice and they said no. She said to call Grandpa and ask him what Grandma's symptoms were when she had her strokes.

I called Grandpa, and I told him some of what had been going on with me for several days and that my voice and speech were messed up and I couldn't make them normal. He said that it sounded exactly like a stroke to him and that I should go back to the hospital. I cried. It was all that I could do. Trying to accept that, even though I was young and had a great job finally, after moving back to Oklahoma, what would happen if it turned out to really be a stroke and not some abnormal side effect of having a little bit higher blood suga

Friday, I couldn't walk at all, or stand without holding on to something. I almost had to be carried if I needed to go just a few steps away. I had to hold onto walls, tables, chairs, counters, or people who were close to me. But I was in denial and chose to believe what the doctors in the ER told me, instead of what I knew deep down was the truth. I wanted to go to Texas and laugh and see my friends and not feel so alone. Steve and I left Friday afternoon.

Everyone was already at NASCAR when Steve and I got to the campsite. They were all so sweet and happy to see us. One of my best friends and roommate after high school lived in Texas and was there with her husband and kids. She came over and gave me a huge hug, and I cried. She knew something was wrong with me. She would have known even if I hadn't started crying.

I found a chair around the fire, grabbed a drink, and talked to friends when they came up. This was the night everyone partied a lot before the first day of the races. But I knew I could not do that, so I told Steve to go and have fun, that I'd be fine where I was. And I meant that, I felt okay sitting by the fire, chatting with people who walked over to talk to me and I wanted Steve to have fun and not feel burdened by me and my strange behavior this past few days.

Steve and I slept in the back of Dave's van, it was nice, pillows, blankets, and a heater in the window to keep us warm. But my sleep since Friday was not good. I could barely move my left side, so I kept trying to move it but couldn't and getting comfortable was hard. I told Dave, Steve, and a couple others that I was going to stay at the campsite during the race, because I knew I could not walk the long walk to the track and through the crowds of people. I had already paid for Steve's race ticket and told Dave he could sell mine. I had also already paid for our part of the campsites, so I didn't owe anything. Dave put me in his camper, so I would be inside while they were at the races on Saturday.

I cried a lot on Saturday, because I was there alone most of the time and only had too much time to really think about things. I liked being independent and able to care for myself, but it scared me to have to depend on anyone else, because people leave when times get hard, they don't try to understand or figure out how to live with someone who is suddenly different. Plus, I did not want to be someone Steve would regret knowing in the future. Steve came back early from the Saturday races and I know it was because he was worried about me more than anything else. But that is who he has always been, he is a guy, but he has a heart and he thinks about how others are feeling.

Steve and I ate, hung out and talked with everyone that night but I went to sleep early since I seemed to get tired constantly. I am not sure when he came to bed, but I only woke up for a minute and I was out again. We both woke up early on Sunday because I was hurting everywhere, my walking was worse, my speech was worse, and I couldn't do anything myself. We decided to go ahead and leave that morning, so we waited for everyone to wake up, ate breakfast and said our goodbyes. To be honest, I don't remember very much about driving home, but I probably slept for most of it until we stopped for gas or food.

Mom called on Monday morning, from Las Vegas, she was visiting April and Kendall. I told her I had gone to Texas, but it wasn't much fun with all that was going on. I also told her what Grandpa had said to me and that I felt like he was right and the doctors at St. John's simply did not want to do the tests on me because I had no insurance. I could not drive either because I could not even walk or use my left hand. Work had also given me leave. Mom said she would be home Tuesday night and would come pick me up and take me to a free medical clinic on Wednesday morning. My job did not offer insurance, and no one would insure me as a Type 1 diabetic. I am not sure if I looked up free medical in Tulsa or if Mom decided where to take me on Wednesday at 7:30am.

By Wednesday, November 10th, it had been 8 days since I had fallen down the stairs and my foot started hurting, and each day following that day things got worse and worse. Mom took me to Catholic Charities incredibly early. I could not walk so she basically held me and drug me to her car, then she had to pick me up and throw me in. I know it isn't funny, but she threw me into the floorboard so many times that even we were laughing at how terrible it was.

When we got to the clinic, white building, green roof, I can't ever forget it, but she came around and helped me get out of the car. Then she held me tight and I tried to step with my right leg and drag my left one, but we weren't doing well at all. The people inside came running out with a wheelchair, put me in, and once we got inside the building a nurse gave Mom a pink piece of paper and said to go straight to St. Francis hospital ER and give them the pink paper, to come back here the Wednesday after I was released from the hospital, and then they would get my information. The pink paper they had given to my Mom said to treat me and Catholic Charities would take care of the cost.

Mom drove me straight to the emergency room, and I cannot remember much, but it was terribly busy and there were patients sitting in the hallway with IV bags attached, because there were no beds. But I feel like they got me in very quickly, put in an IV, checked my blood pressure and said it was remarkably high, put something in my IV to relax me and took me for an MRI. After that, I told Mom to go ahead and go while I was put in a room to wait for a doctor to get the results of my MRI. Mom said she would wait with me for results and then go get Tori from school.

The doctor came in quickly about 30 minutes later. He said they would need to admit me because the MRI showed a massive stroke of my right brain stem. They needed to do a CT Scan and other tests, as well as, bloodwork. I would have to wait some time to get into a room, so Mom left, and I fell asleep.

I do not remember much of the next several days, so I will just tell you the moments I do remember. Mom was coming back up the next day, Steve was going to come up the next day also. I got a room sometime Wednesday evening. I remember Mike and Bobby being the first to come and see me. Mike was my best friend and Bobby was also a close friend, we had all met at our first job at 16, in Owasso. Mike was using a cane and limping but otherwise looked great. They brought me flowers. Mike said he was still waiting on a diagnosis for his leg, and that he still hurt a lot. But he smiled and hugged me and him just being there with me made me feel better. Mike was always the first to be wherever I was, no matter what, to help. Truly a friend like no other.

My Grandparents came up and saw me, they brought me flowers too. I love flowers. We talked for a while, but I can't remember what we talked about. My Grandma and Grandpa are the absolute best in the world. They love me unconditionally and always care. Most of my time in the hospital, I remember crying. I was by myself most of the time, Mom did come every evening, but otherwise, it was me, a ton of tests and shots and thoughts about what I was going to do now, and more and more doctors.

I couldn't walk or move my left side at all. I felt like I was stuck in a very tiny space and I couldn't move. I slept a lot and every time, every single time, I woke up I thought what had happened was all just a bad dream, and I could walk and move again. But then I would try getting up and nothing would move on my left side. It was frustrating and irritating, and I just wanted the use of my body again. I wanted to get out of bed with a smile, take a shower by myself, I wanted to get dressed by myself and brush my hair, wash my hair. I just wanted my life back.

Mom kept telling me that Steve was going to leave me. She told me this ever since I had called her in Vegas and told her something was horribly wrong with me. I didn't want to hear that, it made me cry uncontrollably and I told her he would never leave me, and he seemed okay with what was going on with me. But, in many ways, I think I was simply not ready to think about that part of my life. Could he really leave? Would I blame him?

I was in the hospital for eight long days. They were trying to get me a bed in their rehab wing of the hospital, but it was full. I asked if they could send me home until there was room for me. They sent an Occupational Therapist and a Physical Therapist into my room to evaluate me and teach me some basic exercises that could help me. They showed me how to use a walker and then said they were going to discharge me to my home. They were going to have me do in-home rehab and speech therapy instead of staying in the hospital. I was happy I could go home because I missed Steve and really needed to be near him, it felt like he was the only thing that kept me from just breaking.

Mom drove me home from the hospital and Steve was pulling in at the exact same time. I hadn't talked to him since the day before, he had been busy, I guess. He did not know that I was coming home. He helped Mom get me inside and bring in all my things. It felt good to be at my apartment again, instead of in the hospital that felt cold and uninviting to me. Mom said goodbye and I gave her a kiss and she left.

I still sounded terrible when I tried to talk, my speech was bad, and I hated it. I tried not to talk unless I had to, at first, just because it sounded horrible. I am a talker and I found myself trying to say nothing and just be quiet, so no one would hear me. I also fell many times a day. I had lost any sense of balance I used to have, trying to figure out a walker was difficult too. I could be trying to simply stand, and I would fall over.

I didn't sleep in bed, since it was upstairs, and I didn't know how to do stairs yet. I slept on the couch in the living room, alone. I only got to shower once a week when Mom came over, because she could help me stand, wash my hair, and help me with everything else. I did not have a shower chair then, as I had no idea all the things that would help me.

My rehab therapists started coming out about a week after I had come home. I slowly got my speech back to normal doing exercises my therapist gave me, practicing them every couple of hours, talking slower and pronouncing my words very clearly. I tried talking as much as I could to Steve, to my best friend, Mike, on the phone, and my Mom.

My physical therapist taught me how to climb stairs carefully and in a different way, so that I could sleep in my bed instead of on the couch. She taught me to get down the stairs going backwards to put less pressure on my knees. I was happy for this because I wanted to sleep in bed, near Steve, so I wouldn't cry myself to sleep every night.

I was extremely emotional after my stroke; they had told me it was very normal. I would cry if anyone talked to me, if I saw anyone, if I tried to talk or just tell my work how I was doing. It was terrible, I got used to crying at least every 30 minutes, even if things weren't sad.

I felt very alone in my recovery. Others couldn't really begin to understand how it felt. It took every ounce of energy just to do small things. And there were so many things I couldn't do at all anymore. I could not do our laundry anymore, and that was something I did every Friday night before. I could not cook anymore, I loved to cook before my stroke. If I didn't cook, we would have never had good meals. I could not drive to see my family, drive to visit friends, drive to Steve's shows anymore. Everything changed. I was so young, barely 35, and my entire life was unrecognizable to me. Depending on friends to come and see me, that just doesn't happen. Does not matter how close you are, they will stop coming by. People mean well, but they say they will come see you or go to dinner with you, it just doesn't happen.

It's not because they don't care about you or what you are going through, but they have their own lives, shows to do, work, friends to go out with who can drive and meet them. Life keeps going. This made me feel alone. I tried to hide the sadness as much as I could, even from those close to me. Mom had been telling me since the stroke happened that Steve was going to leave me. Honestly, I couldn't even try to think about that and how I would pay my bills, rent, car insurance, groceries, meds, or anything. I really could not even start to plan for something like that, there were so many things already needed from me.

I slept a lot during the day. It felt like I just could not get enough sleep even if I slept for 15 hours. I hid this, even from Steve, I would fall asleep the minute he left for work and wake up 15 minutes before he came home. Still, I did feel things changing with him. It really wasn't his fault. I still loved him with all of me, completely. I gave as much as I could to him, but I imagine, just after my stroke, I was completely helpless because I could not even walk. So, I did feel him pulling away, and I knew it was partly because of what happened to me, and partially because his Mom was sick in the hospital.

I had no income anymore since I had to stop working after the stroke. My Grandpa and Grandma told me they would pay my portion of the rent and bills until I was approved for disability. Mom paid for my cell phone each month and I was put on food stamps to buy my part of groceries. I had learned, through the many years of dating and being married, and having my sister with me everywhere, how to be independent and not need someone else to be there to pay my bills, work for me, drive me places, cook, keep the house clean, or anything. But I felt so alone, after the stroke, that I was completely dependent on Steve being there. I never felt safe unless he was with me. He went out a lot with friends after work, but I would not sleep until I heard him come in the door. He was the only one who motivated me, encouraged me, and made me keep going to rehab.

It was, as though, everything April had taught me growing up and about how to live my own life, suddenly could not be done anymore. Steve's Mom was extremely sick the entire month of November, which made things excruciating for him. He was working so many hours, doing everything at home, and making sure I had all I needed while he was at work and could reach everything, and trying to go see his Mom as much as he could.

Thanksgiving came, and Steve and I were going to my Aunt Sandra's home that afternoon, but he was going to visit his Mom in the hospital in the morning before we left. Steve hot home around noon and we left for Bartlesville. He never said much to me about how his Mom was doing. I don't remember much from that Thanksgiving, but my Uncle Steve told Steve that he was a good guy and to take care of me. I remember everyone wanting to see me, hug me, and find out what I knew about what had happened to me. It had been 23 days since my stroke on Thanksgiving.

On November 28th Steve got a call, his Mom had died. I knew something was wrong because he said he would be there soon and hung up the phone, and just sat there and didn't move. I quietly asked him what happened, and he said his Mom had died. I started crying. I know that was not the right thing to do, I needed to be the strong one for him right now. I felt so awful, he had just lost his biggest fan. The pain he felt, I couldn't even imagine. I hugged him, he hugged me and cried. He tried to pull himself together a bit and left for the hospital a few minutes later. November was a severely devastating time.

November 29th was the anniversary of my rape, and I know that sounds weird, but it is a day I know each year. It is a dark day; it is always a very cold day. Steve was in so much pain already, that I kept it to myself. It was three or four weeks since I had my stroke, about 2 weeks since I got out of the hospital. I was still doing terrible and never asked for help with any of it. I liked doing things for myself, asking for help with such stupid things was embarrassing and frustrating for me. I liked being in control of my own finances, my work, and my free time. Since the stroke, I felt I had no sense of control over my life or the choices being made for me.

Steve and I had gone to his Mom's home to get a few things, while his Dad was there. His Dad was always so sweet to me. I had only met him a couple of times, but he always was worried about me and my comfort, far more than his own. He was a very warm man. We had already had the funeral for Judy. It was a beautiful ceremony with beautiful flowers everywhere. There was so much love.

Steve got a few things from her home, his Dad gave him her pill carrier and blood pressure monitor, for me. I still use both weekly and every time I do, I remember her. Then we left her home and drove back to Tulsa. We had been getting along fine, no fights or arguments, we hadn't really talked about how he was feeling, he didn't like to talk about things at times, and I would not force him too. I did tell him a few times that I was there if he just wanted to talk about things. Steve never fought with me, I loved him too much to ever need to just fight about anything, and we just seemed to get along.

When we got home that night, we watched TV and didn't really talk too much. As I was getting ready to try to go upstairs, he said that once our lease was up, that he wanted to be single for a while and live alone. It took me by surprise because he had never said anything like that to me before. So, I asked him if he wanted to break up, and he said yes.

I don't remember much after that. I remember not wanting to cry, wanting to be strong and just thinking how this was over and we were stuck in a yearlong lease here. Mom was right, and how would I live without my Steve? I wish I could answer that question, but even now, I can't really answer that question.

I had never had a bad day with Steve for the sixteen months we had gone out. Never an argument that would ever make me feel like I was going to leave, or he was. I could lie to you, say Steve was terrible, a cheater, liar, abuser, or thief. But that would be far from the truth. He is as close to perfect as I'll ever be. He always cared for my heart and gave the best of himself to me. I don't know if any of our relationship was real or true, maybe we were both living a big, fat lie and didn't want to see the reality.

I went on, after my stroke, in an unbelievably bad way. I dove headfirst into sorrow and pain and blaming myself for everything. If there was a light, I never got a glimpse of it. Each day got harder, more painful than the day before. The last piece of me, was now broken into a million little pieces since Steve broke up. I can't explain how I felt, I couldn't breathe, I was suffocating, drowning, dying inside. I felt done with trying to make this life work anymore or believing in anyone in my life. Promises broken, my soul was broken. Steve moved on easily, and that hurt. Steve partied until morning with friends from work, dated, had fun, worked, could drive. It all hurt to watch, and I could do nothing about any of it. I had no way to get away from it.

We tried to figure out what to do about our living situation and Steve was the one who said, we could both still live there, he would help me, and my grandparents and Mom were going to help with my part of things. Everything was in my name in the utilities, so I needed to keep those on track. So that is exactly how it went for the next 10 months.

I longed for my short days to end and my long nights to end, and to find some sense of safety and security in my life. It was always cold when I went to bed, cried myself to sleep in silence, with my ex-boyfriend asleep next to me, why, I am not sure. We were not together, not even in love, just torture to my heart to sleep beside a man who no longer cared for me. Break ups are hard, I know this. But living in the same small space with someone who told you they did not want to be with you, said it had nothing to do with the stroke, but knowing it is over, is difficult. I couldn't date again, and I knew myself well enough that dating would not work for me until I found some reason to get better. The sky had fallen on me, and I was suffocating.

I ended up taking a handful of Amitriptyline one night, knowing it could kill me, but nothing mattered to me. I knew it could kill me because a close friend's wife had died after taking an overdose of hers. I was dizzy and confused and kept passing out, and I had called April, in Vegas, and left a message telling her that any money I had left I wanted Kendall to have. I said I was tired of everything and didn't know how to fight anymore. I fell asleep, asking God to please take me from this darkness and to not let me wake up another day. Steve woke me up some time during the night, and said the police wanted to talk to me. I got up, weak and still very dizzy, probably from the pills. The police had been called by my sister, who had tried calling me, but I did not answer. She called them from Las Vegas and told them she needed them to come check on me. They talked to me and asked why I was so dizzy, I told them my blood pressure was probably low, so they checked it, it was 58/69, which was low, but normal for me on my medications. They asked if I was going to hurt myself, I said no. They left a few minutes later but gave me a card with a number to call the next day.

But I had no hope. No light in my life, nothing to look forward to, but a broken body that could not work, and some bad memories. I slept all day and only woke up for a couple of hours at a time. I had no one to talk to and nothing to live for. Everything was cold and dark and scary.

Steve had been the love of my life, the first serious boyfriend since my divorce in 2008. Friends started telling me they knew he was breaking up, but I never saw it. I still don't see it. All I thought every day, all day, was what had I done wrong to make him want to leave. I had to swallow painful tears so many times. He was trying to date two or three girls at his work, and I was still trying to stop hurting, wondering how it was so easy for him to just move on.

But the truth is, I could not let go. I couldn't get any control over how I felt, how often I cried. Abandoned, isolated, pitied, and sad. That was all there was, just intense pain. Steve still had shows, so they were out late, or he went out after work, so I would be alone from 3pm until 3 or 4am. Utterly alone.

That is when I knew something had to change, and I had to change it. So, I called the suicide prevention number at Family & Children Services. I set up an appointment for help and went three days later. I needed someone to hear about the darkness, the pain, the terrible things I could not get away from. I started going in early October 2011, and still go today in 2018. I was diagnosed with major, manic depression, also known as Bipolar Depression, PTSD, and social anxiety. It took several months to find the combination of medications that helped me. I started packing in October and my family moved all my things in a couple of hours. I was living in an apartment in Tulsa, by myself. Doctors were concerned, Mom was worried, and I was secretly terrified. Steve had moved out earlier in the day, a quick goodbye, and I did not talk to him again for a couple of weeks.

I was not trying to be mean to him, but I had told him that I needed to be left alone for some time, to get over things, and I would try to be his friend again. He had said that he wanted me to always be his friend and promised he would be there for me. But I knew that I would need to be alone for a while.

Mike and I talked almost every night via Skype or Facebook video chats. He was sick. He understood the things I was going through because he was in a wheelchair now and getting ready to stop working so he could try to deal with his illness.

My friend, Matt, and his then girlfriend, now wife, Susan,

came by my new apartment on October 24th. I remember because I had just started on a new anti-depressant that was changing things in me, for the better. I still cried all the time, but
this drug made me want to get out of bed, get dressed, and start
writing again. It wasn't sudden, but it was good and getting better.

So, Matt and Susan came in carrying two pet carriers and
these two little kittens were inside of them. These sweet little
meows were coming out of them. Matt opened the pink carrier
first, and out came this tiny, little kitten meowing and talking
away and exploring my apartment. Oh my gosh, she was so
sweet and fuzzy. She came right to me, and Matt said, "happy
birthday"! She was mine! I named her right away, her name was
Abby. I was going to name my first daughter Abby, but I never
had any children, so she would be my Abby.

I got my first happy feeling that night. She gave me a reason to
get up, to play. It was a feeling I forgot I could have. I took her
everywhere with me, if Mom came to get me, Abby came too.
She loved Mom's house, she loved riding around on my walker,
and she fell asleep every night sucking on my earlobe and pawing my shoulder. Abby has been my light, my rock, my inspiration, and my friend every day since.

So, I felt so much loss and desperation when I did move into
my first apartment, after my stroke. It took so much out of me
just trying to figure out how to live on my own again, and how
to do things differently without the use of one side of my body.
Mike was my best friend and he could no longer drive either. So,
we were both in similar situations back then. His disease was
obviously far worse than mine, because while I could fight and
do rehab and get stronger each year, Mike's disease would end
up taking his life and he would slowly go from walking to not
being able to move his legs, arms, hold his head up, swallow and
so much more. So, in every moment when I would just cry out
loud, I would tell myself I had no right to cry over where I was in
life, when my best friend was going to lose his. We spent hours
texting on the phone or video chatting since he could rarely

have someone bring him out to my apartment and no one could take me to see him.

Mike had ALS; he was diagnosed with it about three months after I had my stroke. But Mike understood how I felt being frustrated, disabled and quite literally, alone. Mike was always there for me, and trust me, I had a few major breakdowns living alone, with no company, no job, and no income. Mike always had such positive things to say, all the time, and he never gave up on life or loving people, even though the disease he had was fatal and he knew he would progressively get worse, no matter how hard he tried to slow it down.

Still, I could tell him anything and everything and he would never judge my feelings or how I got through things. We talked a lot about Steve, and to be honest, it was difficult for me, I couldn't get over Steve. I felt like I was refusing to accept that he really did not love me. I was not the girl who fell in and out of love with a toss of the dice.

I had loved him completely and I was angry with him because he had left at my lowest and most destructive point. When every emotion was super sensitive and scarred me forever. I thought he had left me because I could never be "normal" again. I couldn't just go and hang out at the bar or take camping trips or drive to some little town for the weekend. I told myself that because I couldn't pay for our vacations or trips anymore, that I wasn't any use to him anymore.

Every word he ever spoke to me, every kiss, every look, every laugh and every promise, felt like just another lie, and I wondered if the entire relationship, that I had thought was so perfect, was just one big lie. I was torn between the feelings that I held on so strongly to, for Steve, what was really happening with him even though I didn't want to admit or accept it, and what he was telling me and promising me.

Mike talked to me about these things. I think that I got so much comfort from him because he made me understand that Steve just couldn't handle such a huge loss from his Mom to me. It was just too much for him. I don't pretend that I know this is true, but that thought softened the blow to my emotions. Mike would tell me anger is a bad thing to carry around and that I have no control over what others do in a crisis. Mike was incredibly good at making things make sense to me. We did lots of crying, lots of laughing, every time we spoke it would last for hours and we always ended our talks with an "I love you" and feeling more complete than either of us would without each other.

2011 was a year of transformation for me. I found my friend, Adam, who I had grown up with. We had remained friends through the past 20 years, he was one of those friends I did not see often, but we talked all the time and remained close. I remember Adam so well he is a forever friend. He was a beautiful soul, sparkling eyes, tan skin, mesmerizing smile, and he was just simply a beautiful man. He was tormented by things through the years since school. He worried often about his Mom and her health and had lost his Dad already. He loved his Mom to the moon and back.

He had also been in some bad relationships while I was living in Vegas. But he spoke to me often about one of the relationships that was the best to him, with a girl named Beth. At the time, I had never met her, but he was always telling me he went to a concert with Beth, cooking dinner at her house, they were going out somewhere. He also talked so much about his dog or cat. Adam was an animal lover, so caring and kind. He was just a warm and inviting person.

Truthfully, Adam was insanely beautiful, he was just breathtaking. Adam had called one night and said he really needed a job, so I called Steve and got him an interview with Kim and told him to put Steve down as a reference. Kim hired him, and then 2 days after Christmas he called and left me a voicemail. Before I could call him back, Beth called me at home. She had never spoken to me before, so I was a bit shocked to have her calling me. She told me he had died a few hours earlier, in an apartment fire.

Adam never showed up for work at Hideaway, and I told Steve

that he probably wasn't going to be there, because he had died. I lost one of my best friend's that day and I don't think anyone can console that kind of devastation. After Adam passed, I did open my heart a bit more. I chose to put my anger aside and the outrage I felt. I became friends with Steve, I called him and told him thanks for giving me time and that I needed a friend. He was there for me, not just in trying to handle my friend passing, he also showed me he really did want to be my friend and he was there for me during so many changes in my life, a lot of devastating times and so much internal bitterness.

I could talk all day about my resentment, but none of that would change the fact that Steve did want to be my friend, part of my life. He was encouraging and surprised me. I had wanted to hate him, I had such anger because I had loved him completely and a month after moving in together, I had my stroke and he suddenly broke up with me. I felt as though, my stroke and my health were the reason he stopped feeling love for me. But maybe he was not meant to be my love, our connection seemed so much brighter as friendship.

Steve was a good soul. He genuinely cared, and the negative things said about him, are just my perception of the circumstances at the time. It was not who he was, it was about who I was. It was my anger, my mistrust of him, my pain just from the emotions after the stroke, trying to put a wall between myself and Steve. But I was lucky, I knew that it was something I had to work through in myself, and I could not keep trying to blame him for any of that.

After Adam died, so suddenly, death became unpredictable to me. There was not time to waste on being angry or wanting Steve to hurt as I did, or to have some understanding of my pain. Life flies by, ends with no warning and we only live once. Just once, so we must stop and really think about what is most important in our lives and does it have to be as we imagine it in our minds, or can we still need it exactly as it really is?

Funny how losing a lifelong friend can affect my entire life in a better way. Steve was close to me. He saw things happen to me that I would never share with anyone else in my life. He lived that first year after my stroke working so many hours, shopping, cooking, doing laundry, cleaning up things, and trying to deal with his own losses. His loss was much greater than I could ever imagine and still he never yelled or got angry. He just maintained it all very well.

Steve never broke down, maybe a few times, but mostly not in front of me. He dealt with my single worst year, trudging through this swamp of dark feelings. I was so terrible then; I cannot fathom ever feeling that way again. He saw more of it than anyone else ever would and I don't know why he didn't run. Why he chose to stay and help me through that time I will never know, but trust me, only a patient and very understanding person would have. He has said once during that first year, that he should have run as far as he could, and I would not have blamed him at all for leaving. I was a complete wreck to all those who knew me and especially to myself.

Adam died in December of 2011, and the next year would prove to be just as difficult for me, even on an emotional level. I had no relief from my pain, would not take pain medications because I was smart enough to know how addictive they could be and that I was in a bad state of mind. The anti-depressants helped me not to want to physically hurt myself but made me feel like I was locked in a box, choking on my suffering, resentment, and frustration. I did not want to kill myself, but I still did not want to try anymore either. If I had to live this way for the rest of my life, feeling like this, then I just did not want to live anymore. I felt like my choices had all been taken away from me and nobody would let me decide on anything anymore.

At the end of 2012 I had been living alone for just over a year. Mike was getting worse because of his ALS and I cried a lot after we'd get off the phone at night, just because I could not imagine how he felt or how he still smiled and laughed and loved everything so much. He couldn't eat with his hand anymore and his neck could not hold his head up anymore, but he always loved every moment of living, and I wanted to feel that. He helped me to feel sane and normal, when I was disabled and unable to do so many things at such a young age. He helped with all my anger from Steve, made me still know that angry love is better than depressed love. I was so sick of crying, all the tears, feeling abandoned and like I had no choices in any of my relationships. Mike talked with me for hours, mostly about my heartache and my troubles, even though I know his must have been so much bigger. I was so afraid of what other people, family, friends would think of me if I ever spoke about how I felt. I knew everyone in my life was trying so hard to be there for me, after my stroke, but I had so much pain still. Mike laughed and knew exactly what I meant when I told him that I still hated Steve telling me about his dates or the 20-year-old kiss he partied with. I felt like if I couldn't do those things then how was it fair, he still could? Yeah, I realize that's just stupid, but it really does happen. I always thought about how different it would have been if Steve had left me and I hadn't ever had a stroke. How much easier it would have been to be working, move out, move on, and love another who would not see me and always be concerned with my health. But that would never happen now.

My life had taken a turn over the last two years, from happy and social to having no company, few friends, and no life at all. Mike did not just turn that feeling away, but he made me believe that life could be better my way. He completely understood me like no other person has ever understood me, except my twin sister.

It is true what they say, 'if you want to know who your true friends are, go through something horrible, and see who sticks around.' It's not enough to say you will come visit, go out for dinner, or just go out, especially when you never show up, not even once. But I hurt inside for Mike. They had him on so many medications in 2012, sleep meds, pain meds, pills that helped him eat and swallow, pills to help the depression. Just so many things they had him on, and he still had pain and stayed up all night because he could not sleep.

He could not sleep in a regular bed anymore, so he got a hospital bed that helped for a little while. But it was difficult to transfer him from his wheelchair to his bed or chair. He had home nurses to help him bathe, check his blood pressure, heart, breathing, swallowing and try to help with therapy for his movement. I felt bad that I was getting much better, could live alone, shower, dress myself and eat, and used a walker now to walk instead of being in a wheelchair. I wanted to encourage him; he was my best friend. I wanted to tell him things would get better, but I could not because that would be a lie. He couldn't get better; he could only get worse.   In mid-2012 he had to move into a nursing home in Jenks.

He couldn't risk a fall or choking of food and David and Chelle both worked and couldn't watch out for him 24 hours a day like he needed. I cried for him, being almost 40 and having to live in a home with concrete walls, medical equipment everywhere and no family or friends there all the time. They visited him often and I still talked to him on the phone or video chat at night, but that place did not feel like a home, it felt like a hospital.

Mike always called me his butterfly. The memory of that still makes me smile. In November 2012, Mike got sicker. We still talked but he could only do it for maybe 30 minutes before he had to hang up. He had a flu or cold that they could not seem to get rid of, so he had to sleep most of the time. It lasted almost four weeks, he said he just hurt all over. It was in his cheat and he said it felt like bronchitis or strep throat. I emailed Chelle in late November to ask her to please let me know if he got worse, got taken to the hospital or anything, because I knew this disease would kill him and I promised Mike he would never be alone in his final moments, that I would be there with him. That seemed to be his only fear, that he would die, and no one would be there. He cried a lot at the end of November 2012, always telling me he felt so lonely and didn't want to be alone. So, I told him he is always and forever in my heart and if he feels alone to just think of me and know that I am right there next to him.

It was right after his birthday December 5th, that I got a call that he was taken to the hospital. He had gotten worse, the hospital said he had pneumonia and he could barely breathe. Chelle called me and said the doctors said we should come to the hospital because he was bad, and they did not think he would make it. So, I texted every friend I had to find a ride to the hospital, because my Mom had already gone to Tulsa to eat dinner. I needed to hurry, I made Mike a promise that I would be there, and I wanted to always keep that promise. A guy I had dated in early 2012 answered his phone and said that he would drop me off.

I got there about an hour after Chelle had called me. I had to walk an exceedingly long way because Don dropped me off at the opposite end of the hospital and I had no idea. I finally made it to the right elevators, got to his floor and started looking for his room. I passed the nurses station and saw him for a moment in a room right across from them. But the nurses said I could not go in and see him yet because the doctor was in there. They said I could go in, in a few minutes but that his family was down the hall in a room on the right. So, I walked down the hall to find David and Chelle.

I finally found them in a small waiting room with a friend of Mike's. I can't remember who she was, but I believe she was one of his home nurses. Chelle saw me first and said hi, and I said hi back and came to sit down with them. Then she said that Mike died ten minutes ago. I started crying, trying to be quiet, but my crying was uncontrollable. She said the doctor thought he had a stroke in his sleep and never woke up. All I kept thinking was that my best friend had died, and I was not there with him. I was in the hospital, but with my walker since my stroke, I was terribly slow, and I never made it to him in time. I felt so much pain inside from not being able to keep my promise to him, my best friend who only needed one thing, one thing he was afraid of, being alone. My best friend was gone, gone forever. I could never hear his voice, hug him, hear him laugh or give me advice … never again.

I called Bobby, one of our other friends since high school, who was also close to Mike. We had all worked together at our first job, that is how we met. He said he was driving to the hospital but just had not made it yet. He showed up about ten minutes after Chelle had told me about Mike. I remember he was smiling and wanted to go see Mike. I had to tell him Mike was gone, and I do not think I have ever had to give someone such horrible news of a friend before. I was crying so hard trying to tell him, and he just kept asking me if I was serious. Then he hugged me as a nurse came in and said we could go and see Mike, that he was ready.

Bobby went with me to see him. I saw Mike in the room, he looked like he was sleeping. He looked calm and peaceful. But I knew he was gone because usually when he saw me, he smiled big and wanted a hug, first thing. This time, he did not smile or ask for a hug, he did not wake up at all.

I think that would be the day that I stopped putting all my faith in God. Not that I don't believe in the possibility of him, but I felt like if he could put a disease like ALS into the body of a man who meant so much to so many, who had lived true and inspired every person who met him, if he could be evil enough to poison such a beautiful person then I did not want to be part of his world.

Mike would be mad at me for that. Mike was one of the best people to ever be in my life and he should not have gone so young. Thinking back on that moment, that day, makes me break. I called and told Mom, she said she was so sorry, and she would go to his funeral with me. My family loved Mike, they all knew him very well, knew about his illness and he used to visit me at Mom's, or she would drive me to see him in Jenks.

Mike had donated his body to ALS research so his picture was at his memorial instead. I had sent him beautiful flowers, and Mom and my younger sister, Shauna, both took me to his funeral. I dislike the word funeral, it is heavy, so we can call it his celebration of his life and memories.

They played Mike's favorite song by AWOLNATION, Sail. I

had introduced him to them and played that song first. Then they played our song the Crow and the Butterfly by Shinedown. Mike always said I was his butterfly, and this would be our song. Friends and family got up and spoke, told memories of Mike and funny things they had done together. Both of Chelle and David's kids got up and spoke about Uncle Mike, he loved everything about those two. So, hearing them made me smile. I was crying so much that I chose not to speak. I loved Mike, he knew, I knew, and they all knew. Mike was the chicken and I was the clown at Hardee's at our first job. So many memories there.

After the service, Chelle gave the painting he had Mom paint for him, that he had designed, and hung in his room in Jenks. His painting still hangs on my wall in my living room today. On my bookcase, is a picture of Adam. Two people who passed way too young. Two very dear friends to me who died in terrible ways but will always be alive inside of me.

I am unsure if I could begin to show you the immense ache and emptiness inside of me after losing my friends. I do not know how I will go forward without either of them here, but I will. Life had purpose with them here, I had a place. And I will be sure to give others a place in this life and a purpose, for them, this will be my reason for doing life to the fullest.

So, the last three years of my life were tough. A divorce, move to Oklahoma, met Steve, had a stroke, Steve left, lost two best friends and somehow, I was still standing. I could lie and tell you I handled it all well, but that would be laughable. I didn't. It felt like being pushed underwater and fighting for just one breath, being pushed under again and continuing this over and over and over again. I ended up toxic to myself and anyone who tried to be close to me. At least that's how I felt and tried to not be around anyone so I would not ruin their lives too.

There was a time when I was sweet, kind, fun, happy and beautiful. It seems like a million years ago. But my friendship with Steve grew stronger. He seemed to take the place of my lost friends. Not sure he intended to, but he was strong for me and always there. Steve filled a huge void in me, he also told me what I needed to hear and not what I wanted to hear. He was honest, no frills, straight to the point and supportive. Steve has become a far better friend to me than when we were together as a couple. Steve liked to tell me to chill out, I would be fine, write a little and chill out.

Steve became my best friend. After I put away my selfish feelings, my anger, and thought about Steve's own struggles and loss, I became better and open to letting him be close to me. I started getting used to being alone a lot, my awkward way of walking and my ways. My sister, Shauna, was going to have her first baby in May of 2014 and I was feeling good. I knew myself better now and accepted myself and started enjoying my own company. I learned how to care for myself, not need a relationship because I may never have that again, and to be happy with the love I had.

I am ok with where I stand with life now. We cannot plan out our lives, things will always happen when they want to happen. Get good with yourself and be ready to change with the circumstances. I have accepted that I will never know what will happen next in life. I may never get married again. I won't be able to have children. I may never fall in love again. But I do know I will not hide what I feel or want from anyone again. I will absolutely be the best I can be for others in my life.

There is a struggle every day, not nearly enough support for the emotional loss and loss of independence from a stroke. I must fight myself at times, to be okay with what my life is now, not to feel unable to do what I love or to feel good enough to live. But I am good enough. I live by a line in a song I heard in early 2011 called Kill your Heroes, "never let your fear decide your fate". I live daily by that now.

William Henry Johnson, Jr.

Gender: Male   Alias: Billie Johnson
Race: Black   OK DOC#: 244828
Height: 6 ft 1 in   Birth Date: 11/13/1963
Weight: 250 lbs.   Hair Color: Black
Eye Color: Brown   Reception Date: 5/28/1996
Current Facility: MACK ALFORD CORRECTIONAL CENTER
Case Number: 95-5796

Crimes: RAPE BY INSTRUMENTATION - 15 Y
            KIDNAPPING – 10 Y
            REC/POSS/CONC STOLEN VEHICLE – 7 Y
            ROBBERY – 45 Y
            RAPE – FIRST DEGREE - LIFE

Don't Blame Me

What was I wearing, did I lead him on?
What was I thinking to drive him around so long?
Did I try and fight him, or did I give in?
If I had fought harder, did you think I might win?
Why couldn't I run and why couldn't I scream?
You think I exaggerate and go to extremes.
STOP!!! Stop and listen, do you hear what you say?
Do not tell me you know what I went through that day.
Did you feel the sting of his fists hit my face?
Did you feel the chill of the night and that place?
Did you feel my fear, as I felt the death?
As he lay over me, could you smell his soured breath?
You could not have felt this...and it is just too late for advice
For that night lost my innocence, and I pay that price.

Inside of Me

The purest form I ever saw
a ray of light so blind to all
She came so quickly and so fast
we knew this innocence would not last
so plain and simple, as she could be
she was the angel inside of me
A broken wing she shall not fly
no questions asked, no reason why
a hope, a vision...this she gave
for our lives she longed to save
A beautiful smile and sparkling eyes
she keeps in silence all her cries
To give a world what she can
to put her spirit into the soul of man
such subtle truth in her word
listen close to what is heard
she came along and changed our place
she came, a shadow with no face
just a warmth I can't explain
washed away with the rain.

Who Am I?

I stand here, naked and frail
showing you my scars, my pain, my tears
I curl up here on the floor and wonder
if my fears are because of you
or if they are because of man himself
I am here before you, showing you all of me,
opening my soul here for you ...
wondering what do you see?
Do you want only what you see in clothing
in makeup, in jewelry...
do you want the dirt and the tragedy,
the sin and the regret?
do you see me, or do you not see me at all
I stand here naked and alone, unprotected,
will you warm me and accept me ...
or am I just a body made for sin,
and not a soul and a heart with pain and tears
and love and life inside of me
standing before you,
who am I?

He Never Even Knew Me

He never even knew me.
I was just in the wrong place
I thought he needed help from me,
and he had such a sweet face.
He just seemed so nervous,
always on the edge of his seat.
I couldn't see through the darkness,
and I began to get cold feet.
He really seemed quite stupid,
and soon he had me lost.
I thought, "I'd like to call a cab for him
no matter what the cost."
The streets were dark and quiet,
and I had no clue where we were.
I felt the knots inside my stomach,
and my intuitions stir.
But I tossed aside the worries
and thought, "It's just silly me."
This poor guy needed someone's help;
this is where God wants me to be.
We stopped at a convenience store
so, he could use the phone.
I thought he should call his sister
because we couldn't find her home.
I looked around the parking lot,
and God, I so wanted to go.
I had so many choices then,
but I just didn't know.

I saw him, he was coming back,
and I just held my breath.
He said, "She's only a mile away."
Thank God there's just one mile left.
Back on the street, so dark and cold.
Man, I didn't like this street.
There was a sign, what did it say?
I felt so tired and so beat.
I was confused, it couldn't be,
did the sign say what I thought it said?
I asked him, "Did that sign say, 'Dead End'?"
Was that what I had read?
Inside I felt so sick and scared,
as I tried to turn around.
I hoped I could get out of this,
still there was no light to be found.
He kept telling me to watch it
or we might end up in the ditch.
I wished he'd sit back and just shut up,
because all he did was bitch.
I finally had the car turned around
so, I could go back to the store.
Let his sister come and pick him up,
because I could take no more.
And that's when it happened,
as I tried to get my car to go.
He slipped it into neutral,
and I didn't even know.
Such fear rose from inside of me,
but I tried not to let it show.
But when I saw into his eyes,
the fear began to grow.
I tried to drive away again,
when his hand grabbed my wrist.
"Oh God, no! Is this happening?"
I saw him make a fist.

His eyes looked crazy through the dark,
the only thing that I could see.
Through a night filled with blackness,
was this happening to me?
A blur of pain and darkness,
a fear so deep and strong
A haze of blood and silent cries,
in a night, my life went wrong.
The golden thread of life, which held me,
and bound me to a world, so cold
Broken, when he beat and raped me,
and the tragedy unfolds.
My breath slowed, and my body
just went limp, I lost control.
I didn't cry. God, was I dying?
I can't describe all that he stole.
He threw me on the frozen ground,
and he kicked at me some more.
I guess he figured what the hell,
what else is she good for?
When he thought he took my life from me,
and I was close enough to death
I heard him as he rushed away,
and still I held my breath.
When the car had been started,
still on the ground I laid.
The grass my warmth and blanket,
so, there is where I stayed.
When those two taillights had faded,
I slowly lifted up my head.
The fear inside left me shaking.
'God, could I be dead?'
I didn't know if he'd be back,
so, I got up and tried to run
I had to find a place that's safe
from what this man had done.

He never even knew me;
I was just in the wrong place.
He made me feel sick inside.
I couldn't look him in the face.
It's not the end of the story,
oh no, there's so much more
I found a house to go to,
but they wouldn't open up their door.
Please, someone help me,
please don't let this man come back.
I promise not to scare you,
but I know he will be back.
The next house opened up their door
and quickly pulled me inside
Covered up my naked body,
which I quickly tried to hide.
I made it through the terror,
but my fear is always there
I could never forget the feelings
or the pain that I must bare.
I know my life's worth living,
but sometimes when I'm alone
I realize some things I go through;
I must go through on my own.
And no one knows my losses
because they are simply mine
Other survivors understand me,
and our stories, somehow are intertwined.
He never even knew me;
I was just in the wrong place.
My intuitions told me,
now I will never forget his face.

Updates

So many people have helped me along the way, and I love each of them for helping me through these times. I mess up a lot in the things I do, but I love you and care about you all, no matter what. My life would not be the same without each one of you as a part of it.

Never forget how very much I love you all. You can always remember me through this story if we should lose touch. I know it felt really good to write this even though it was hard sometimes and has taken many years. Thank you for making me the person that I am and for giving me the courage to face the new challenges of life.

Today is January 15th of 2003. It has been more than seven years since my rape. I never thought in a million years that I would be able to live a life as full as I am living today. Even just a year ago, I thought that my rape would always leave me with something missing in my life. I did not think the memories would ever fade away. But today I feel differently. While the memories of the rape still linger in my mind, they have become a part of my past and not my future. I have been blessed with a beautiful niece, a wonderful boyfriend, a great job, and a comfortable home.

I have learned to appreciate those things that I once took for granted, like a smile of a baby, or the phone call from my sister or my mom. I have grown wiser with knowledge and figured out what it is that makes me happy. Love doesn't disappear when you are raped. Love shines all around you in the faces and hearts of family and friends, and all the wonderful people who stand by you no matter how hard it gets. Wow, is my family strong or what?

The stranger did not steal my life away. He did not take my soul. He may have confused me and made me think I had misplaced it, but I am still here. I am still as caring and understanding as I ever was. I know now that I have made it through. I am now a survivor and I have my family and my friends to thank for helping me to realize that.

Today it is February 27th of 2012. What can I say, it has been 17 years since the rape. There is a reason for everything. I am still alive and that is more than I should be by all accounts. I still can't read this book without crying. Remembering how life-changing that moment was, and now knowing how it was and will always be just one of the trials & difficult times I will always remember with a lot of pain. I have never felt before the intense burning pain in my heart that I have felt this past year. I suffered a severe stroke of my right brain stem on November 2, 2010 at the age of 35. It is still so painful and overwhelming for me that I cannot write about it, because for now I cannot face those memories. In another book, I will. But not now!

Now I just feel like my higher power obviously needs me here. People have been removed from my life because they were not good for me. But in return, through it all, I see the absolute beauty in others, in simple things like the sun, the wind, the music around me, and the unconditional love of family & friends!!

Acknowledgments

MOM, you were the first to hear of my assault and the first to stand beside me throughout the first months of my recovery. Because of you, Mom, I am alive and happy. You have given me so many reasons to go on and to be better than I am. You keep me dreaming and believing in myself. You are the best friend that I always needed and the Mom that others only dream of. I love you.

APRIL, thank you for always being there. You came to the hospital and you will never know how much that meant to me. I love you and could never imagine living my life without you. You will never know how much you have meant to me over the years of my life, and even though I never tell you like I should, I love you so much.

TORI, because you are the innocence that we all wish we had. Such a sweet smile and beautiful girl. I could hug you all day and night. I love you and am so happy to have a brand-new reason to live. You will always be my Tori Bear.

SHAUNA, thank you for being my sunshine. You are my guardian angel. You probably don't even realize it, but you are the one I thought of when I was so sick and when I felt so low. You are the one who always made me know I had a reason to be here. It was your face that I would see when I thought my life was ending, and it was you in my memories, that made me feel okay. You are far more beautiful and special then I think you realize. I love you sweetie.

HOWARD, thank you for being the light of my mom's life. You have made her entire world shine again and I can't even tell you how much that means to us all. You are one terrific guy. Thanks for understanding when I needed her to be close to me and thank you for your patience.

SANDRA, thanks for talking to me about what happened and for always giving me hope and comfort when I needed it most. You are always good to hang out with and you keep everyone laughing and smiling. Good luck in your new marriage. I love you.

GRANDMA and GRANDPA, thank you for helping Mom so much and for the understanding, love and support in my recovery, trial, and future. I love you both so much and I want you to take care of yourselves. I miss you.

LISA and JAMES FREDERICK, thank you for my life. Thanks for the great friendship and the open heartedness you both possess. You will both be lifelong friends and always in my heart. You made the biggest difference in my life and I will not forget you. I love you guys.

ERIC STALL and ELIZABETH O'NEAL, thank you for helping me to heal from my ordeal. Without you both, Johnson may never have gone to jail. Thanks for the hard work, the patience and understanding with me, and for being such special people.

DETECTIVE RICK SHEA, thank you for giving me strength and helping me to believe in myself again. Thanks for working so hard on my case and for supporting me. You inspired me so much. You are always in my heart.

MIKE B., thank you ... just thank you for the smiles, the hugs, and the unconditional love & friendship. You are always in my heart and soul.

TROY, thank you for being a great friend and giving me someone absolutely wonderful to hang out with while living in Las Vegas. You are a very spiritual and beautiful person and I hope that you can become everything you want in this life. I love you.

OMA, you are thought of each and every day. I will hold you in the most special of places inside of me and I pray you are laughing, and I know you are in a good place.

ADAM GILCREASE, those phone calls when I would not leave my house, thank you for believing in me and never once leaving my side. I wish you had told me sooner about the bus ... I know I can always count on you, and you can always count on me, I promise! And you know me and a promise!!

STEVE, we didn't meet until 2009, but we both know we were so meant to be in one another's lives. You literally broke me out of a place I never want to remember. You showed me what it was to have a love that was always honest and truthful, even when it hurts. You never failed to be the one who stood by my side and pushed me through my recovery. You saw the very worst side of me and the absolute best. Mostly though, you love me so much, as only a true friend could, and I will always love you.

KENDALL, you are my sunshine. Since the day you were born, my life was changed. You are the sweetest little thing in the whole world and April and Aaron are so lucky to have you. I love you sweet Kendall.

AMELIA & DAWSON, you both will forever be my "littles". I have loved you since before you were born and even more after. You both completely make my heart smile and feel whole. Love you two, always.

STEVE & TRACY, you both are very loved and your support throughout my life is amazing. Thank you for being my family. Mike and Me 2012

Mike and Me - 2012

Adam

Steve and Me

Kendall

Abby, my baby

Mom

William Henry Johnson, Jr.

BA Man Gets Life, 45 Years for Rape, Robbery

By Bill Braun

World Staff Writer

A Broken Arrow man was sentenced Tuesday to life plus 45 years in prison for raping and robbing a Tulsan who gave him a ride from a convenience store.

William Henry Johnson Jr. committed "aggravated and egregious" crimes against a young woman who tried to help a stranger, said Assistant District Attorney Eric Stall.

Johnson, 32, pleaded guilty to five felonies — first-degree rape, rape by instrumentation, kidnapping, robbery by force, and possessing a stolen car.

Johnson pleaded guilty to three misdemeanors — assault and battery, attempting to elude a highway patrol trooper, and operating a defective car.

Tulsa District Judge Clifford Hopper sentenced him to consecutive terms of life plus 45 years in prison as part of a plea agreement reached after a jury had been selected for a trial.

"I would like to apologize to all parties," Johnson said. "She didn't do anything wrong. I was the one in the wrong. It's my fault and I accept complete responsibility for it."

At a Jan. 19 preliminary hearing, the woman said she stopped at a store at 41st Street and Garnett Road around 12:30 a.m. Nov. 29 and was approached by Johnson, who asked for a ride to a relative's house in Broken Arrow.

She testified that while she was driving and following Johnson's directions, he hit her several times.

Johnson said Tuesday he then drove her to an area by a Broken Arrow sports complex, where he raped her.

Stall said Johnson "dumped" her away from the car before driving off alone.

The woman was able to identify Johnson as her attacker. Police said Johnson could be identified on videotape taken by a surveillance camera at the convenience store.

About 24 hours after the attack, a state trooper saw the car — with one headlight out — being driven on Pine Street. After a pursuit, the car — driven by Johnson — stopped after running out of gas at 11th Street and Lewis Avenue, according to reports.

The life term allows for a possible parole. Hopper also ordered Johnson to pay $4,600 in fines and victims compensation fees.

McVeigh's Mom Speaks Out

FORT PIERCE, Fla. (AP) — The mother of Oklahoma City bombing suspect Timothy McVeigh denies her son was part of any organized militia.

"I have been silent up until now because I am a private person with a private life," Mickey Frazer said in a letter hand-delivered to The Tribune of Fort Pierce-Port St. Lucie. The newspaper published the letter Tuesday.

"Only time will tell the outcome of what really happened in Oklahoma City on April 19, 1995. Many initial reports and leaks have been changed, denied or are unsure.

203

About The Author

Angela Parker

I am 44 years old. I live in Owasso, Oklahoma now, but I spent almost 12 years in Las Vegas, Nevada. For fun, I love music, listening to it at home, live at a local hangout, and in concert. I also love kitties. Especially my baby girl, Abby Abster, who is now 9 years old.

I wrote this book for many years. I started in 1996, and as different things happened in my life, I wrote more in order to recover and understand things. I could not read the story of my rape for many years; it was too real. It simply gave me so many nightmares and memories. I was finally able to read it in 2014, and chose to share it with others, hoping I could help others who were scared, or family and friends, who needed to understand.

Books By This Author

Shattered Pieces

The original book I wrote about my rape & trial.

This Is My Life

This book is about my stroke, mainly. It gives a little about my life from 21 years of age until now.

A Life Of Poetry

A book of poetry I have written since 1985

Shattered Pieces A Compilation

This is my latest, combining the story of my rape, kidnapping, stroke, and my life up until now. There are also a couple of poems written after, and about, my rape

Made in the USA
Coppell, TX
03 May 2024